Our_Sovereigns_From_Alfred_To_George_Vi

Osbert_Lancaster Osbert_Lancaster

CONTENTS AND ILLUSTRATIONS

The dates after the Sovereigns' names represent the years of their reign

CONTENTS

The portraits of the Monarchs, with the exception of Edward VIII and George VI, in this book are reproduced from the original collection assembled by the Proprietors of ENO'S " Fruit Salt " for the Monarchy Chart with which they commemorated the Silver Jubilee of King George V.

FROM Alfred to George VI the English throne has been occupied by no less than fifty-four sovereigns. Their lives and deeds have been exhaustively investigated and frequently chronicled, and some knowledge of their careers is the property of every schoolboy. Their likenesses, however, are, save in a few outstanding cases, less generally familiar, and those monarchs who were not so fortunate as Henry VIII and Charles I in possessing either a distinctive appearance or a genius as court-painter, have frequently come featureless down the ages, or still worse, wearing masks not of their own devising. Thus the unfortunate little Edward V is known to many of us only through the romantic medium of the talented M. Delaroche's highly imaginative art, and to the older generation of playgoers the features of Henry V are for ever those of the late Mr. Lewis Waller. With the coming of the cinema this process of substitution has notably increased, and even those kings whose appearance is familiar to all are now in danger of undergoing a slight but subtle metamorphosis ; thus Henry VIII (already, one gathers, known to the youth of central Europe solely as " Ein berühmter Filmkönig ") has developed a strong likeness to characters so diverse as Rembrandt and Captain Bligh, and his dominating personality seems likely to merge as completely into that of his skilful impersonator as has L'Aiglon's into the late Sarah Bernhardt's.

The purpose of the present volume is to present in a compact and accessible form a collection of portraits of all our kings reproduced from contemporary originals. These pictures are of varying merit, but all were painted either during the lifetime or shortly after the death of the sitters, who thus appear to us as they did to their contemporaries. Some, such as the splendid head of Henry VII and Lawrence's dashing sketch of George IV, are works of art of a high order; others derive their whole interest from their subject.

Of their accuracy as portraits one can only judge, in those cases where no corroborative evidence exists, by discovering how easily one can reconcile what one already knows of the monarch's character with the traits discernible in his features; a highly subjective proceeding as unreliable as it is entertaining. However, while there is nothing easier than to read into a face vices or virtues which we are already aware from other sources that its owner possessed, it is surprising how frequently the appearance of our sovereigns fulfils the expectations aroused by a knowledge of their character. The weak, furtive but not unintelligent features of Edward II as he is here portrayed must surely be regarded as providing further proof of those failings which history tells us involved him in his downfall, and all Richard III's ruthlessness and cunning are made credible when one regards his portrait. Occasionally the artist reveals a side to his sitter's character with which we are not always so familiar; for example, in the portrait of Henry V. That small full-lipped mouth, that long inquisitorial nose provide striking and unexpected support for the belief that the gallant warrior-king was both bigoted and persecuting; characteristics of which, curiously enough, one looks in vain for any traces in the charming features of Bloody Mary. (This particular portrait, however, was painted when Mary was still quite young; her later pictures reveal only too clearly how fearful a change was wrought by illness and misfortune.)

With regard to those pictures which have been taken from tombs, Henry II, Richard I, John and Henry III, one can make no definite claims, for not everyone is agreed that funerary monuments such as these are to be regarded as portraits in the strictest sense of the term. However, there is no evidence that they are not, and one is justified in supposing that the artists possessed at least some familiarity with the royal features. That of Henry III, for instance, not only portrays a man whose character would, one imagines, resemble closely that of the King as it is described by historians, but also displays a strong family likeness to the portrait of his grandson. How far our earliest kings resembled the pop-eyed grotesques who appear on their coins remains a matter for conjecture, but one can assume that these numismatic caricatures are at least far more like the originals than those self-consciously noble and heavily hirsute figments of the nineteenth-century historical imagination which used at one time to appear in all the popular history books.

To each of these portraits has been attached a short biographical sketch, giving some account of its subject's career and character. These have been founded on the usual sources and are in no case the result of original research. The object of the author has not been to interpret afresh the course of our history, but solely to provide a short summary of the lives of our kings. If occasionally a personal bias is discernible, it arises from a conviction that the characters of some of our monarchs have been as heavily romanticized by the popular imagination as have their features by the artist and the film-producer ; it is no iconoclastic urge which has led him to emphasize, in one or two cases, those personal failings which our schoolmasters were always at such pains to ignore, but rather a desire to emphasize the fact that the institution of monarchy rests on so firm a foundation that it can always survive not only the vices and idiosyncrasies but also, as recent events have so clearly demonstrated, the personal popularity of individual monarchs. In an age of intense publicity and foolish propaganda, temptation to descend to the level of the film star and the dictator is very strong, and we may be thankful that it presented itself at a time when the throne was occupied by a sovereign who preferred rather to renounce his rights than to yield to its deception. For popularity has its dangers as well as its advantages, and the more easily it is won the more easily it is lost. Moreover, it is a significant fact that those kings who are the most dearly loved at their death were seldom remarkably popular at the time of their accession and both Victoria and George V ascended the throne without arousing the enthusiasm of their subjects in any very striking degree.

At a time when so many varieties of government are springing up overnight, it is suitable that some consideration should be given to so ancient and so successful an institution as the English Crown. Of the fifty-four monarchs who have worn it, a small number have been rulers of genius, a few disastrous incompetents, but the great majority have been neither the one nor the other, but simply men and women of widely differing character whom the accident of birth had placed on the throne and who contrived, partly by luck and partly by judgment, to remain there. Few of them were so gifted as Oliver Cromwell, but few were less regretted; a point which should be borne in mind by all dictators, for fantastic and illogical as the hereditary principle may seem it provides a supernatural sanction, involves an act of faith and establishes a continuity. While personal dictatorships imply a very large measure of faith, racial purity is but a poor substitute for the ceremony of coronation and the question of the succession remains unsolved; republics, on the other hand, while they are founded on a more immediately rational basis and frequently achieve a somewhat shaky continuity, make no spiritual demands and history has shown repeatedly that nations can no more live by bread, or logic, alone than can individuals. It is therefore a matter for the most profound gratitude that the English monarchy has survived so many dangers, has adapted itself to such a variety of changing conditions and rests to-day on such firm foundations. Particularly should we be grateful to those sovereigns whose reigns covered a period in which the Bourbons, the Braganzas, the Romanovs, the Hapsburgs, the Wittelsbachs and the Hohenzollerns all vanished from the European scene, and who yet succeeded in passing on to their successors a crown for which they had secured by their conduct a prestige and a popularity of which history affords us no other example, and to that monarch who preserved these hard won advantages by abdication, when it became clear that the compromise that would have secured his private happiness was likely to have dimmed their lustre.

1937.   O. L.

The direct line of descent from Alfred to George VI

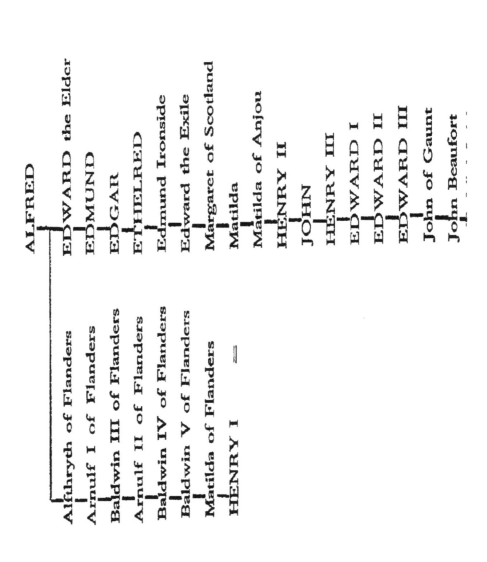

ALFRED

EDWARD the Elder
EDMUND
EDGAR
ETHELRED
Edmund Ironside
Edward the Exile
Margaret of Scotland
Matilda
Matilda of Anjou
HENRY II
JOHN
HENRY III
EDWARD I
EDWARD II
EDWARD III
John of Gaunt
John Beaufort

Alfthryth of Flanders
Arnulf I of Flanders
Baldwin III of Flanders
Arnulf II of Flanders
Baldwin IV of Flanders
Baldwin V of Flanders
Matilda of Flanders
HENRY I =

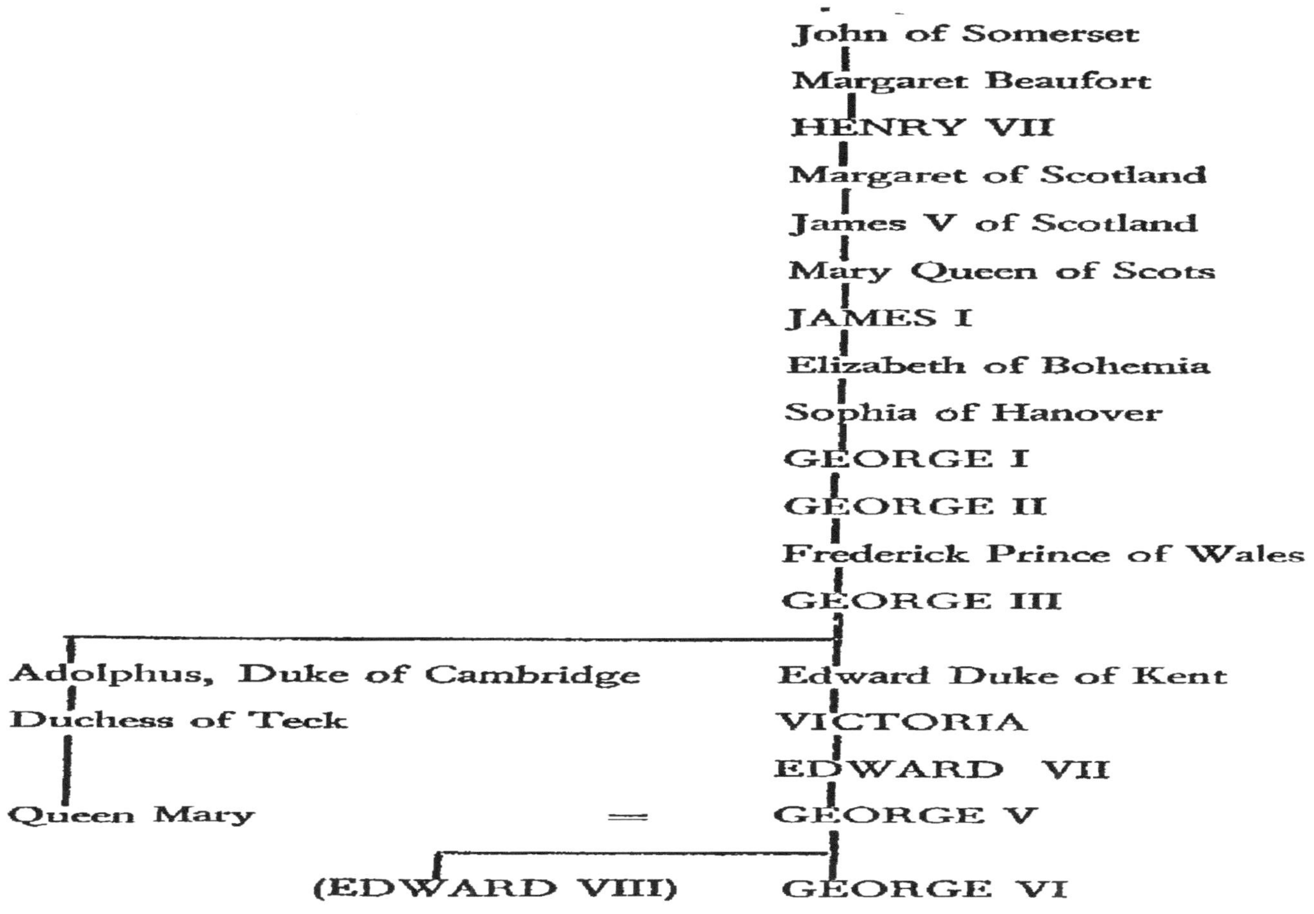

John of Somerset

Margaret Beaufort

HENRY VII

Margaret of Scotland

James V of Scotland

Mary Queen of Scots

JAMES I

Elizabeth of Bohemia

Sophia of Hanover

GEORGE I

GEORGE II

Frederick Prince of Wales

GEORGE III

Edward Duke of Kent

VICTORIA

EDWARD VII

GEORGE V

GEORGE VI

Adolphus, Duke of Cambridge

Duchess of Teck

Queen Mary = (EDWARD VIII)

ALFRED
871-901

EDWARD THE ELDER
901-925

ATHELSTAN
925-940

EDMUND
940-946

From coins in the British Museum

ALFRED THE GREAT 871—901

AT the beginning of the ninth century of the Christian era the ,chief threat to the recently attained, and still comparative, tranquillity of Western Europe came from the war-like tribes of Scandinavia. As these barbarians were a sea-going people, it was those countries with a long and exposed coast-line who suffered most from their depredations. England was doubly unfortunate, for its political as well as its geographical situation caused it to fall an easy prey to the ravagings of these Norsemen. At this time the country was divided into seven separate kingdoms whose mutual jealousies prevented them from forming a common front against the alien menace, and by the middle of the century the heathen Danes had established themselves all over eastern and northern England.

In the year 871 there succeeded to the throne of Wessex, Alfred, the grandson of that Egbert who had made his kingdom the most powerful in Britain, and is the ancestor of all our subsequent kings with the exceptions of Canute, Harold, and William the Conqueror. (As the last of these married Matilda of Flanders, a direct descendant of Alfred, the blood of Egbert was reintroduced into our Royal Line and his present Majesty is his descendant in the thirty-seventh generation.) This determined and courageous young prince not only succeeded, after many years of almost continuous warfare,

I   B in driving the Danes out of his own kingdom of Wessex, but also forced them to conclude a peace whereby his territories were considerably enlarged. As soon as he had brought the war to this successful conclusion he proceeded to devote all his energies to repairing the ravages which his dominions had suffered for so long. A staunch believer in the supreme value of education, he brought over from the continent numerous scholars and churchmen, caused a variety of religious and instructional works to be translated into the native tongue and codified his country's laws. Realizing that the first line of defence against the enemy was on the sea, he created and equipped a strong navy, which fully proved its usefulness when the country was next menaced by the barbarians. Moreover, having himself twice visited Rome, he was fully alive to the significance of international events, and was the first English King who was justified in regarding himself as a European monarch and not merely a provincial potentate. Although many details of Alfred's life remain obscure, quite sufficient is known of his actions to warrant his being surnamed the Great.

EDWARD THE ELDER 901—925

ALFRED was succeeded on his death in 901 by his son Edward, commonly called the Elder. This prince inherited much of his father's energy and ability and his first action on coming to the throne was to suppress a rising of the Danes of East Anglia who had acknowledged Alfred as their overlord but seemed disinclined to do the same for his son. A few years later occurred a second rising of the Danes, and when, with the aid of his brother-in-law, the overlord of Mercia, Edward had completely defeated the rebels, he incorporated their territories in his own kingdom of Wessex. On the death of his sister Athelflaed, her principality of Mercia descended to Edward, whose dominions were thus once more enlarged. In 924 he received the homage of the Kings of Scotland, and in the next year he died, leaving his son Athelstan a realm such as no English king had ever before possessed.

ATHELSTAN 925—940

ATHELSTAN was fully as able and energetic a man as his father, and he immediately devoted himself to consolidating his vast but rather loosely held dominions. On the death of one of his vassals, the Danish king of York, he dispossessed this prince's heirs and took his kingdom for himself, whereupon he found himself faced with an indignant and powerful confederation of minor princes which included the Kings of Ireland and Scotland together with numerous bands of Danes. These enemies he completely defeated at the great battle of Brunanburgh, and as a result of this victory Athelstan became the undisputed overlord of the whole of Britain. Alfred had raised his country to the status of a European power ; his grandson made England the strongest and most respected nation in Western Europe. Before he died in 940 Athelstan could count among his brothers-in-law the Emperor, the Kings of France and Arles and the Counts of Paris and Flanders.

EDMUND 940—946

HE was succeeded by his brother Edmund, a youth of eighteen whose energy and courage were well displayed in the promptitude with which he overcame two risings which occurred early in his reign, one of the Northumbrian Danes, the other of the Welsh who at that time inhabited a part of the Scottish lowlands. Doubtless Edmund would have proved a worthy and efficient king, but unfortunately he was assassinated during a banquet by one of his drunken thegns, after he had filled his high position for less than five years.

EDRED
946 955

EDWY
955-958

EDGAR
958-975

EDWARD THE MARTYR
975-978

From coins in the British Museum

WITH the accession of Edred in 946, there opens a new period in the history of the House of Egbert. Hitherto our kings had all approximated to the hero-type, completely overshadowing even the most exalted of their subjects of whom we hear little ; now various minor figures begin to emerge from the background of court life, which has itself become sufficiently sophisticated to provide an atmosphere in which plottings and intrigues can freely flourish. Edred was a pious but delicate man who devoted himself with great energy and considerable success to the task of absorbing into the bulk of the nation the numerous foreign, chiefly Danish, elements in the population, who had hitherto led a life apart while giving their allegiance to the English King. In carrying out this admirable policy he was ably assisted by St. Dunstan, the Abbot of Glastonbury, a wise and energetic man, whom, had he not received the dignity of canonization, one might hesitate to acquit of pride, ambition, and complete unscrupulousness. Like so many of his race Edred was doomed to an early death, and he had not occupied the throne for ten years when he was succeeded by his nephew Edwy (955).

EDWY 955—958

THIS unfortunate young man (for Edwy was only seventeen at the time of his accession) soon made the discovery, as did two other English kings after him, that to have a saint at court, although gratifying to one's pride and notably increasing one's prestige abroad, entails numerous disadvantages. For consideration of the feelings of others is too seldom a saintly characteristic, and Dunstan proved no exception to the rule. For some obscure psychological reason this great man took an extreme dislike to Edwy's young and beautiful wife Elgiva, and never let slip an opportunity of abusing her to her face. Not unnaturally Edwy retaliated by banishing the saint together with many of his supporters. However, Dunstan was more than a match for the wretched Edwy, and soon returned in the train of the King's younger brother Edgar, whom he had encouraged to take up arms against his sovereign.

EDGAR 958—975

AFTER a short period of civil war Edgar was sitting on his brother's throne with Dunstan standing at his right hand; and Edwy had vanished from the scene with a mysterious but convenient suddenness.

Now that his own protégé had become king, Dunstan could concentrate all his energies on the reform of the

English Church which had long been one of his favourite projects. During the Dark Ages, Ireland had been the greatest centre of Christian learning and activity in Western Europe, and although it was now in communion with Rome it had retained, and to a certain extent transmitted to England, certain doctrines and rites of its own with which Rome was not wholly in sympathy. On this subject Dunstan held views which to-day would be regarded as ultramontane; in particular was he anxious to reform the English Monastic establishments along the strictest Benedictine lines. Needless to say his zeal, and it must be admitted his tactlessness, aroused considerable opposition in the English Church, which had hitherto been practically autonomous, and although while Edgar lived he was in a position to enforce his views, from henceforth there were two parties in the land.

Edgar himself was a capable and pious ruler, though slightly ostentatious; on one occasion he had himself rowed up and down the River Dee by six of his vassal kings. His private life, despite his well-known piety, seems on occasion to have given rise to considerable comment. However, whatever his moral failings, they were generally attributed, by his logical and patriotic subjects, to the influence of the numerous foreigners who thronged his court. He ruled his kingdom with a strong hand, and alone of all the kings of the house of Egbert he could claim that during his reign the peace of the land was never once disturbed by warfare, either foreign or civil. Like the majority of his predecessors he died young, and was succeeded in 975 by his elder son Edward.

EDWARD THE MARTYR 975—978

AS soon as Edgar was dead his court was involved in plots and intrigues ; Edward, who was still a mere boy, was supported by Dunstan and his adherents, but a strong party gathered round his half-brother Ethelred and his mother, Queen Ælfthryth. The opposition to Dunstan's ecclesiastical policy, which had been latent during the last reign, now broke out afresh, but the saint was no longer in a position to deal with it so firmly, and when the young King was murdered at Wareham by the command of his stepmother, the days of Dunstan's greatness were finally over. Of Edward the Martyr's character and actions little is known, and he must be numbered with " those whose names are justly revered among men but whose works are known only to God."

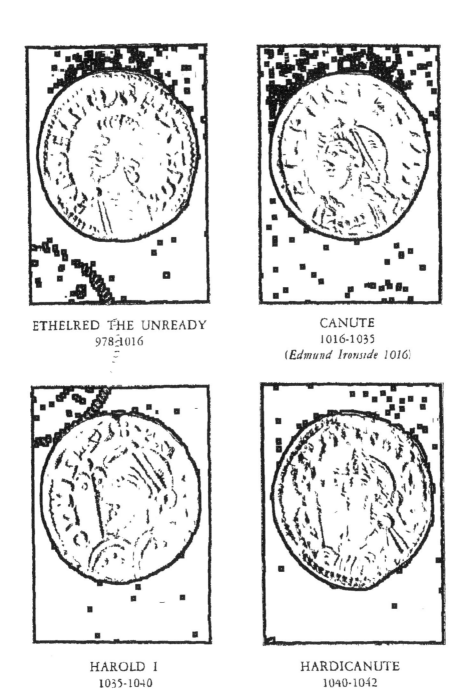

ETHELRED THE UNREADY
978-1016

CANUTE
1016-1035
(*Edmund Ironside 1016*)

HAROLD I
1035-1040

HARDICANUTE
1040-1042

From coins in the British Museum

ETHELRED THE UNREADY
978—1016

HAVING removed her stepson Edward, Queen Ælfthryth had no difficulty in placing her own son Ethelred upon his half-brother's throne. Dunstan himself so far relented as to place the crown upon the young man's head, but characteristically did not fail to avail himself of the opportunity provided by the coronation ceremony for giving tongue to prophecies of the direst woe ; prophecies of which the aged saint did all that lay in his power to ensure the fulfilment. The surname by which the new King is generally known had not quite the same significance for his contemporaries as it has for us ; for them the word meant " ill-advised," but " unready " is equally descriptive in both its ancient and its modern sense of the character of Ethelred. This unfortunate King was quite incapable of dealing with either the dangers which threatened the land within, or the revival of the Danish invasions from without. So great a reputation for strength and courage had the Kings of England latterly enjoyed, that the Norsemen had avoided the country for many years, preferring rather to harass the dominions of less resolute monarchs, but now that the throne was occupied by one of such notorious incapacity as Ethelred, they once more turned their attention to these shores. The earls and magnates whose duty it was to defend the coasts, and over whom the King was quite unable to exercise any effective control, were far too busy quarrelling among themselves to take up arms against the invader, and Ethelred was forced to adopt the fatal expedient of bribing the Norsemen to discontinue their attacks. Needless to say, this catastrophic policy only encouraged the Danes to further onslaughts, and the King thereupon decided upon another and still more calamitous line of action. On St. Brice's Day, 1002, he caused all the Danes resident in England, many of whom were peaceable citizens who had been here for many years, to be massacred in cold blood. Unfortunately for him among the victims was the sister of Sweyn, King of Denmark, and from henceforth Ethelred was no longer faced with the isolated descents of pirate bands, but the organized attack of the whole strength of Denmark. City after city fell into the hands of the invaders until eventually in the campaign of 1013 London itself, which had hitherto always held out against the most desperate attacks, surrendered; whereupon the wretched Ethelred fled to Normandy, and the great council of the nation chose Sweyn as king. Unfortunately the new King died immediately after his election, and as there was considerable opposition to his son Canute, Ethelred returned from abroad and a condition of civil war prevailed until the latter's death in 1016. In the place of Ethelred his supporters chose his son Edmund Ironside, who, although he displayed all those qualities in which his father had so conspicuously been lacking, was unable to hold out against Canute and was forced to come to terms with the Dane. They agreed to divide the country between them, but before Edmund had an opportunity to demonstrate his skill as a ruler he was murdered by a treacherous follower, whereupon his subjects elected to be ruled by Canute.

CANUTE 1016—1035

CANUTE was a wise and able ruler, and, had his successors been more gifted than they were, might have been the founder of a great Northern Empire, for his dominions included Denmark, Norway, Iceland and parts of Ireland, as well as Britain itself. Unfortunately his offspring were quite lacking in the ability and farsightedness of their father.

HAROLD 1035—1040

HARDICANUTE 1040—1042

ON his death in 1035 his son by his first wife, Hardicanute, took Denmark, while England fell to the lot of the son he had by Emma, widow of Ethelred, Harold by name, who ruled for a few years. On Harold's death in 1038 Hardicanute came over from Denmark and appropriated his half-brother's domains, and, in order to consolidate his position and avoid future trouble, took the precaution of assassinating Harold's other half-brother Alfred, the child of Emma and Ethelred. He was an unpopular and tyrannical ruler whose arrival had been welcome to none save Earl Godwin, the great Lord of Wessex who had held the south of England for Hardicanute even during the reign of Harold.

After the new King had misgoverned the country for four years he collapsed in an apoplectic fit at the wedding feast of one of his followers, and soon after died, unregretted and unmourned by the great majority of his subjects.

EDWARD THE CONFESSOR
1012-1066

From the great seal in the British Museum

EDWARD THE CONFESSOR
1042—1066

IT so happened that at the time of his death Hardicanute had staying with him his half-brother Edward, the son of Æthelred and Emma, who had long been resident in Normandy. As Hardicanute himself had no children this pious, middle-aged prince was now the nearest and most acceptable heir to the throne to which he was promptly elected by the Witan or great council of the nation. Being a nervous man, Edward took steps, before accepting the crown, to ascertain the probable attitude of the most powerful of his future subjects, Earl Godwin, who might possibly have been inclined to oppose the coronation of the brother of the unfortunate Alfred, in whose murder he was generally suspected of having had a hand. However, the astute Earl made no objection to Edward's assumption of the royal dignity, well knowing the weak character of the new King, which would the better enable him to continue his control of affairs in the coming reign.

During the long years he had spent in his mother's country, Edward had not only acquired many of the manners and characteristics of a Norman, but had also formed close friendships with many of the most prominent men of that duchy, more especially such as were in Holy Orders. Now that he had become King of England he had not forgotten his old friends, and numbers of them were promoted to rich livings and appointments in his new kingdom. Not unnaturally this influx of foreigners was bitterly resented by his subjects, and it was doubtless with the idea of placating national opinion that in 1045 he married Earl Godwin's daughter Editha. However, as the pious Edward had taken an oath of perpetual chastity, and was moreover a most conscientious man, the chances of the beautiful Editha presenting him with an heir were distinctly remote. The predominance which this marriage assured the family of Godwin aroused the enmity of many of the nobles, including even those who had been gratified that the King should have married a Englishwoman; Godwin and his five sons were now in possession of the whole of the south of England, and this further access of influence was regarded as being dangerous to all. While Godwin's eldest son Harold was a just and upright young man, two of his younger sons Tostig and Sweyn were brutal and overbearing, and the domineering way in which they took advantage of their great position caused the most widespread resentment; the latter was several times banished for outrageous offences, only to be recalled each time through the intercession of his all-powerful father, and reinstated in all his possessions. However, it was not the disgraceful behaviour of his sons that was the ultimate cause of Godwin's downfall, but a dispute with the King in which he might quite reasonably have expected to have been accorded a large measure of popular support.

In the year 1051 there arrived in England Eustace,

Count of Boulogne, on a visit to his brother-in-law King Edward. This prince travelled with a large body of Norman retainers who, while staying at Dover, aroused the fury of the townspeople by the insolence of their behaviour. There followed a disgraceful brawl in which many of the foreigners were killed, and which forced the Count to fly for his life. When he eventually reached his brother-in-law's court he lost no time in complaining of his treatment to Edward, who promptly ordered Godwin, in whose territory Dover was situated, to ravage the unfortunate town as a punishment and an example. This the great earl refused to do, and when he found that he could not rely on sufficient support from his followers to enable him successfully to defy the King, he fled abroad together with his son Harold.

Now that Godwin had disappeared there was no one to check Edward's pro-Norman activities, and the country was soon seething with discontent. But the earl and his son had not gone far afield, and in 1052 they returned with a large fleet, and finding little opposition soon sailed up the river to London. They were at once reinstated in all their dignities, and numbers of the King's foreign advisers were sent into banishment. The next year the old earl died, and from now until the end of the reign the country was governed in fact, if not in name, by his son.

In 1057 there arrived in England Edward the Exile, the only surviving son of Edmund Ironside, who for many years had been living at the court of the King of Hungary. Unfortunately this last adult male representative of the house of Egbert, whether from the effects of his long journey or the sudden change of air, died two days after he had set foot in his native country, leaving only an infant son to succeed him. Thus when Edward the Confessor died a few years later, having just completed his most permanent memorial, the Abbey of Westminster, the question of the succession was still far from any satisfactory solution.

HAROLD II
1066

From the Bayeux Tapestry

O N the death of Edward the Confessor the Witan were faced with the problem of deciding between the rival claims of four different candidates for the crown, of whom no less than three declared that they had the late King's vote. Of these Edgar the Ætheling, the infant son of Edward the Exile, had the most legitimate claim as the last male descendant of Egbert, but the council still retained vivid memories of the disasters that were apt to occur when a minor succeeded, and set aside his rights on the grounds of youth. Another possible candidate who had claimed at one time to have had the support of Edward the Confessor, was Sweyn Estrithson, a nephew of Canute, but he had long ago abandoned his rights in order to contest the kingship of Denmark. There remained Harold himself, whose sole claim, other than merit, was that the Confessor had expressed on his death-bed a wish that he should succeed him, and William the Bastard, Duke of Normandy, whose rights were far more tenuous and complicated. This last was the cousin of the late King, whom he also stoutly maintained had promised him the crown, and had married Matilda of Flanders, a direct descendant of Alfred the Great. But far more important in his eyes than these remote and far from exclusive rights was the promise that he had extracted some years previously from Harold himself.

In the year 1064 Harold had been so unfortunate as

to be blown out of his course while sailing in the Channel and driven on to the shores of Normandy. Here he was detained by the unscrupulous William, who did not hesitate to indicate to his unwilling guest that unless he took an oath to assist his host in obtaining the crown of England on the death of Edward, his chances of ever returning to his native land were decidedly remote. The unlucky Harold was forced to yield to this outrageous blackmail, and swore a great oath in the presence of all the witnesses whom William could produce that he would support the Duke of Normandy's candidature to the best of his ability. However, the right to nominate the successor to the crown, as Harold was probably well aware, lay ultimately with the Witan, and when this body was at length called upon to do so, they showed no hesitation in setting aside William's claim and declaring Harold king.

The council had made a wise choice, for not only had Harold already given abundant proof of his abilities as a ruler, but had also demonstrated in his successful conduct of a war against the Welsh that, granted favourable circumstances, he was not lacking in the military ability necessary to defend the country against the inevitable invasion from Normandy. Alas, favourable circumstances were denied him, for he had not long been crowned, and was preparing to organize his forces to resist William, when he was called upon to face a new danger from quite an unexpected quarter. His worthless brother Tostig, jealous of Harold's royal position, had come to a treacherous arrangement with Harald

Hardrada, King of Norway, who now proceeded to invade the north of England with an enormous army. Harold hastened north to defend his kingdom, and, despite the fact that his forces were largely outnumbered and that the King of Norway was the most celebrated warrior of his age, who had had experience of warfare in countries so remote as the Byzantine Empire and Russia, completely defeated the invading host and slew both his traitorous brother and the great Harald Hardrada himself.

Meanwhile, however, William had not been idle. Not only had he collected a great army from all over Europe, but he had obtained the Pope's blessing on his enterprise, an advantage which had not indeed proved difficult to get, as His Holiness had long nursed a private grudge against the Archbishop of Canterbury, Stigand. Now he took the opportunity of Harold's absence in the north to land his forces in the south of England. Harold hurried back from the scene of his recent victory and, with a tired and sadly depleted army confronted the Normans in the neighbourhood of Hastings. The ensuing battle was long and hotly contested, but at length the superior numbers and equipment of the Normans (they were well supplied with cavalry and archers, both of which the Saxons lacked), gave them the advantage, and when night fell Harold and the flower of the Saxon army lay dead upon the field.

WILLIAM THE CONQUEROR
1066-1087

WILLIAM OF NORMANDY, whose title of Bastard was now exchanged for that of Conqueror, was, in many respects a self-made man. Although his father, Robert the Devil, had been at great pains to have his only son declared legitimate, when William succeeded at the age of eight his enemies were both numerous and powerful; but by his pertinacity and strength of character he eventually overcame them all and had at length made himself the supreme ruler of his turbulent dominions. Having now completely annihilated the Saxon forces at Hastings he marched on London where he received the submission of the principal citizens and was crowned on Christmas Day, 1066.

William was a just though heavy-handed ruler and had every intention of providing his new kingdom with an efficient and equitable government, but he was severely handicapped in his efforts by two serious disadvantages. First, he was quite unable to speak a word of English and was thus frequently led through ignorance gravely to offend against the national susceptibilities of his new subjects, whose customs he was genuinely anxious to respect; second, he was under the necessity of providing estates for his companions in arms, many of whom owed him no personal allegiance and had merely consented to lend him their aid on the understanding that they would be suitably rewarded in the event of victory. However, although he was bound to repay the services which had been rendered him, William had seen sufficient of the trouble in which the monarch whose vassals are too powerful is soon involved, to reward his followers on too lavish a scale, and was careful to arrange that the vast estates of many of the Saxon magnates who had fallen at Hastings should be divided up among a large number of Norman nobles. Moreover, he stipulated that all freeholders should do homage for their land direct to the King and not through a series of overlords ; thus the feudal system, as it was introduced into England, differed considerably from that prevailing on the continent.

During the first few years after the coming of the Normans numerous risings took place in various parts of the country, but owing to the complete inability of the Saxon leaders ever to achieve the smallest degree of co-operation, no difficulty was experienced in suppressing them. To prevent their recurrence the Normans, who were the foremost military architects of the time, built castles at all the strategic points in the land, so massive in construction that many of them have survived until to-day. By 1085 the country was sufficiently quiet for William to undertake his most considerable work of organization, the compilation of the Domesday Book. Every acre of land and every building and every domestic animal on it had its value assessed and was duly noted down in this vast body of records. Bureaucracy had made its first tentative appearance.

The next year William was taken ill and was some time recovering, whereupon the King of France was heard to remark that 'the fat man was long a'lying in.' William, whose excessive corpulence must frequently have given rise to similar coarse jests, on hearing of his brother monarch's humorous outburst, wittily replied that he would do his churching in Paris and thereupon departed to ravage the French King's dominions. While so engaged he was unfortunate enough to sustain severe internal injuries from an accident on horseback and soon after died (1087).

William I, though ruthless and unscrupulous, was a just and exceedingly capable monarch who gave the country which he conquered an administration far more efficient than any which it had enjoyed for many years. Unlike so many of his contemporaries he was never wantonly cruel, and the numerous hardships which the country suffered after the Conquest were in most cases due to the rapacity and savagery of many of his adherents. Had the King been less stern the lot of the conquered would undoubtedly have been far harder.

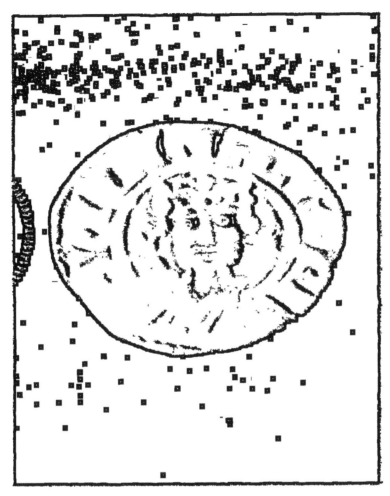

WILLIAM RUFUS
1087-1100

From a coin in the British Museum

WILLIAM THE CONQUEROR was survived by three sons, Robert, William and Henry. On his death-bed he had bequeathed the Duchy of Normandy to the first and England to the second ; to the youngest, Henry, he left only £5,000 with the shrewd comment that Henry had only to exercise patience in order to acquire the dominions of both his brothers. The dying King was under no illusions as to the characters of his sons, of whom the eldest had, even in his father's life-time, given abundant proof of his hotheadedness and lack of balance. William, although far abler than his elder brother, was lacking in that firmness of purpose and political sagacity which Henry had inherited from their father. He was a vainglorious, complex and rather pathetic character who, although he seldom suffered from the effects of his many rash acts, frequently found that his successes proved barren and unprofitable. There was a pointlessness about many of his actions that indicated that he was a man quite devoid of purpose and he seems to have derived little satisfaction from the achievement of his various ambitions.

At the very beginning of his reign he was faced by a dangerous insurrection led by his uncle the wicked and unpopular Bishop Odo and supported by his brother, Duke Robert who claimed the crown by right of primogeniture. William was always at his best in an emergency, and acting with both coolness and promptitude had no difficulty in defeating the rebels. With the restoration of peace the real troubles of the reign began, for William was exclusively a man of action, and when the need for action had passed his character at once began to deteriorate. At first the Archbishop of Canterbury, a clever Italian named Lanfranc who had been the invaluable minister of William I, exercised a restraining influence, but on his death in 1089 there was no one to shield the country from the disastrous effects of William's rapacity and extravagance. In order to finance the numerous wars in which he constantly indulged the people were bled white by taxation, numerous bishoprics and rich livings were sold for cash, while others were never filled at all and their revenues diverted to the royal pocket. From the campaigns against the Scotch and Welsh the country undoubtedly benefited, but no profit was derived from William's endless wars with his brother for the possession of Normandy. In the short intervals of peace the King devoted himself to pleasures that were even more reprehensible and hardly less expensive ; in his vices he was commonly reported to have displayed a sophistication of which his life affords no other example. He may possibly have been, as his contemporaries declared, the very pattern of eleventh-century chivalry, but while he was undoubtedly *sans peur* he was far from being without reproach.

In 1091, during a fit of piety brought on by a severe illness, he at last filled the Archbishopric of Canterbury which had been vacant since the death of Lanfranc and the revenues of which he had for the last four years appropriated to himself. The new Archbishop Anselm was a man widely celebrated for his piety, who only accepted the dignity with the greatest reluctance, well knowing that to curb the excesses of the King was a task well beyond his powers. For some years he stuck to his post despite the constant and sordid financial squabbles with William in which it involved him ; at length, however, even his exemplary patience gave out, and he fled to Rome where he remained for the rest of the reign.

In 1096 Robert of Normandy departed for Palestine on the first Crusade ; in order to raise the necessary funds for this adventure he had pawned his duchy to his brother William before leaving for the modest sum of £6,666. So for the rest of his reign William had the control of Normandy in his own hands, thus attaining by a rather shabby financial transaction the object which so much expenditure of military energy had failed to gain him. Four years later, while hunting in the New Forest in the company of his brother Henry and some few boon companions, he was mysteriously shot dead by an arrow at a time when he was separated from the rest of the party. Whether some peasant had taken his revenge for the enclosure of his lands in the royal deer-park, or some friend turned traitor or whether Henry's well-known patience had at length been exhausted will never be known. The lack of curiosity which his contemporaries displayed in the death of the Red King was only equalled by the restraint with which they mourned him.

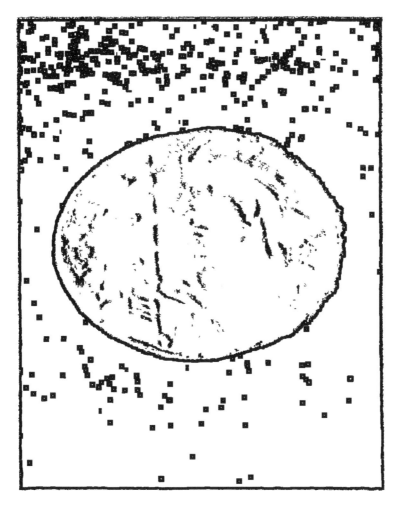

HENRY I
1100-1135

From a coin in the British Museum

HENRY, as soon as he had ascertained the fatal result of his brother's regrettable mishap, took immediate steps to secure the crown, and get possession of the royal treasure. Indeed, so promptly did he act that he was safely proclaimed King long before the majority of his subjects were aware that their late sovereign was dead. Henry was a hard, efficient man with much of his father's ability and none of his brother's foolhardiness and eccentricity. His position in England was far stronger than that of either of the two previous monarchs, for not only had he been born in this country, but he had also married an English princess, Matilda, daughter of Malcolm, King of Scotland, and granddaughter of Edward the Exile. William's death had occurred at a fortunate moment for him, as Robert, Duke of Normandy, had not yet returned from the Holy Land where he had been offered, but had refused the kingdom of Jerusalem. Henry was not so optimistic as to suppose that Robert on his return would be either slow in redeeming his duchy or eager to acquiesce in the assumption of the English crown by his younger brother, and so at once set about preparing to defend his recent acquisition.

Having won over public opinion by remitting many of the taxes which William had levied, by filling up the vacant bishoprics and by recalling Anselm, Henry was in a sufficiently strong position easily to crush a rebellion of his own barons in favour of Duke Robert that broke out in 1102. While he was thus consolidating his power at home he induced the penurious Robert, who had found crusading an expensive occupation, to drop his claims in England in return for a small financial consideration; needless to say, he had every intention of bringing the dispute to a far more satisfactory and permanent conclusion as soon as he should be in a position to resume hostilities. His organizing ability was such that he had not long to wait and in 1106 he invaded Normandy and completely defeated his brother at the battle of Tenchebrai and brought the unfortunate Duke back to England where he kept him in close confinement until his death many years later. Despite the fact that Robert's son, William Clito, continued, with the aid of the French King, to uphold his father's rights until his death in 1128 and kept the Norman frontiers in a constant state of alarm, Henry's dominions were never again in serious danger of invasion. Having settled his affairs on the continent Henry now turned his attention to Wales, where the Normans had hitherto been unable to penetrate very far. He now conquered the southern part of that country where he built numerous castles and installed a large colony of industrious Flemings.

About this time Henry's happiness was shattered by a tragedy in his own family. His only son William was drowned in a storm while returning from Normandy to England, and Henry was faced with the gloomy prospect of being succeeded in a realm which, although it was now at peace, still needed a strong man to direct its destinies, by his daughter Matilda, a princess whose first husband had been the Emperor Henry V, and who, on his death, had married Geoffrey the son and heir of the powerful Count of Anjou (1127). However, Henry was determined, although England had never hitherto been ruled by a Queen, that his kingdom should only be inherited by his own flesh and blood, and at the time of his death in 1135 he had taken every precaution against his daughter's succession being in any way upset.

Henry's rule, although stern and harsh, was of inestimable benefit to England. Not only did he completely abolish all the abuses which had rendered his brother's reign so intolerable, but he sternly suppressed all attempts at independence on the part of the barons. In ecclesiastical matters his attitude was firm but conciliatory; having received an exceptionally good education he was able to meet his prelates on equal terms, and while disagreeing with Anselm on the question of investiture, he was sufficiently tactful to avoid an open breach and a satisfactory compromise was arrived at. The greatest achievement of his reign was the improvement in the relations between the Normans and the native bulk of the population; the King's example in marrying a native princess was widely followed and, from henceforth the nobility tended less and less to regard themselves as an alien and superior race. This happy development was largely due to Henry's inflexible determination never to make any distinction between

Saxon and Norman, and the encouragement he gave
his barons to sever the remaining ties which bound them
to their fatherland and to accustom themselves to regard
England as the future centre of all their interests.

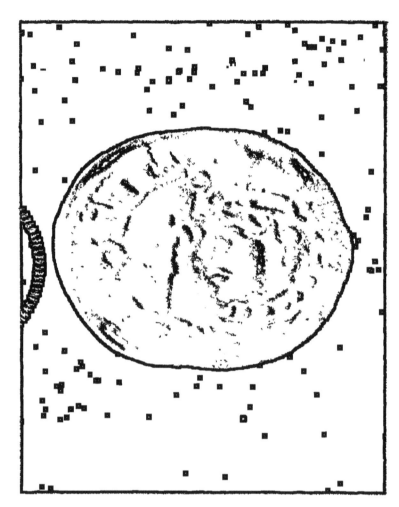

STEPHEN
1135-1154

From a coin in the British Museum

THE most intelligent and efficient of William the Conqueror's several daughters was Adela, who had been married to the Count of Blois, by whom she had had two sons. The younger, Stephen, who inherited much of his mother's intelligence and appears to have had considerable charm, a quality with which few of his family had so far been overburdened, spent most of his time at his uncle Henry's court, where he was generally popular and where he married the sister of the Queen. He seems to have been both prudent and observant, for when his cousin, Henry's son and heir, set out on his fatal voyage to England, Stephen, after taking a look at the crew and the ship, declined to accompany him, and thus preserved his life. He was, however, weak and easily persuaded, and on the death of Henry consented to accept the crown despite the fact that he had twice sworn to respect the rights of his cousin Matilda.

At first all went well, for Stephen was well known to and liked by the majority of his subjects, whereas they knew little of Matilda and far too much of her husband, Geoffrey of Anjou : but it was not long before several of the barons, whose activities the late King had been accustomed mercilessly to suppress at the first sign of any attempt at independence, realized that Stephen lacked the firmness and ruthlessness of his uncle and took the opportunity to build themselves strongholds all over the country which they then proceeded to terrorize at their pleasure. In 1138 the cause of Matilda was espoused by her uncle, King David of Scotland, who invaded England with a large army, but Stephen, although he was in some ways an ineffectual character, had inherited much of his grandfather's courage and military skill and totally defeated the Scots at the battle of the Standard. The next year he was faced with a rebellion of his own subjects led by a natural son of the Conqueror, Robert of Gloucester, and supported by the Church, whom he had rashly antagonized by his cavalier treatment of several insubordinate bishops. Against these new foes he failed to repeat his Scottish success, and when, soon after, Matilda landed in England, the King's forces were routed at the battle of Lincoln and Stephen himself fell into the hands of his enemies : whereupon Matilda proclaimed herself Queen and took possession of London.

The new Queen failed signally to endear herself to her subjects, who were soon so incensed by her haughtiness and the heavy taxation which she immediately imposed that she was chased out of the capital within a few months of her arrival. The cause of Stephen was now taken up by his wife, Matilda's namesake, and the country was henceforth ravaged by the armies of two infuriated Matildas. Stephen's wife was at first so successful that she was able to obtain the release of her husband, but her party gained no further triumphs of a decisive nature and the civil war dragged on. With the collapse of the central authority the country soon sank into a condition of anarchy from which the barons alone derived any benefit : safe in their newly erected castles they changed their allegiance from one side to the other as often as it was to their advantage to do so, they levied what taxes and tolls they pleased and carried on numerous private wars among themselves. At last, in 1153, a truce was made whereby Stephen, in return for Matilda's abandonment of her claims, promised to make her son, Henry of Anjou, who had arrived in England to take up his mother's cause, his heir. The next year the unfortunate King died, worn out by nineteen years' continuous strife. He had many engaging qualities and was well known for his courage and fairness and, moreover, he had never lost the affection of his subjects, but his tragic career only goes to prove that, for a monarch, popularity and charm are seldom enough.

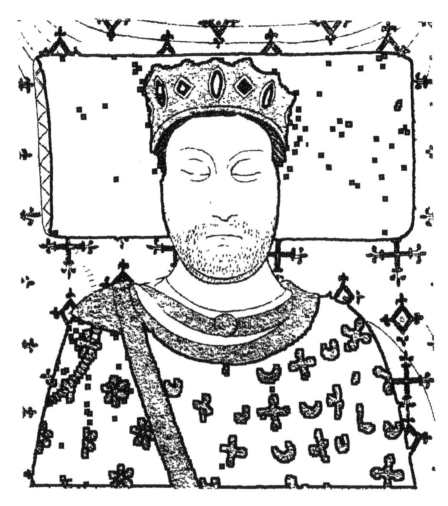

HENRY II
1154-1189

From his tomb at Fontevrault

HENRY II 1154—1189

THE young King who now inherited Stephen's war-weary domains was already one of the most powerful princes in Christendom. His father, whom he had succeeded as Count of Anjou, had long ago possessed himself of the unfortunate Stephen's Norman Duchy, and when Henry in 1152 married the greatest heiress of the age, Eleanor of Aquitaine, he became the undisputed lord of a far greater portion of France than the French King himself. Moreover, he derived more than merely territorial advantages from his marriage, for Eleanor of Aquitaine was not only the richest but easily the most remarkable woman of her times. Her first husband had been Louis VII of France whom she had accompanied on the Second Crusade, where her presence had done much to undermine the morale of the troops and her enormous baggage train had considerably reduced their mobility. The very personification of the great cultural renaissance of the twelfth century, she achieved a degree of emancipation which even modern women might well envy. During her married life with the unenterprising Louis she is reported to have bestowed her favours on a variety of knights, including Henry's father, Fulk of Anjou, her own uncle Bohemund of Antioch and even on the celebrated Saladin himself. At length the French King's patience had become exhausted, and he divorced his exceptional Queen, whereupon she promptly married

Henry, who considered that her enormous inheritance was ample compensation for her various moral
lapses.

On his arrival in England Henry at once set about
restoring order. By reason of the large force he brought
with him from the continent the barons, who had been
playing havoc with the country's welfare for the last
nineteen years, were in no position to offer any effective
resistance when the King proceeded to demolish their
castles and confiscate the booty which they had collected
during the previous reign. In order to guard against
any recurrence of lawlessness, Henry now set about
reforming the administration of justice and instituted
the system of itinerant judges which was the origin of
the modern Assizes. Having pacified his new kingdom,
Henry turned his attention to the continent, where he
soon embarked on a war with the French King for the
possession of Toulouse. With this campaign England
had no direct concern, and Henry allowed his English
vassals to substitute a payment of money for the
customary fulfilment of their feudal obligations, thus
introducing an important modification in the feudal
system. In 1162 Henry took a step that was to have
important and unfortunate results some years later;
he appointed as Archbishop of Canterbury one of the
ablest and most devoted of his ministers, Thomas à
Becket.

For many years the relations of Church and State had
been growing more embittered throughout Europe.
Hitherto England had escaped any definite rupture,

largely owing to the skill and forbearance of Henry I;
but during the long years of anarchy in Stephen's reign,
the Church had remained the one stable institution in
the country and had emerged at the end with its position
considerably strengthened. The new Archbishop was a
man of overweening ambition who in many ways bore
a striking resemblance to St. Dunstan, but unfortunately
for him Henry in no way resembled either Eadred or
Edgar, and very soon a dispute arose between these two
dominating characters over the question of the Church
courts. It had long been allowed that the Church had
the right to judge in its own courts all offences against
the canon law such as blasphemy and bigamy, whether
committed by priests or laymen, but now Becket put
forward the indefensible doctrine that all priests had the
right to be tried before the ecclesiastical courts, no matter
what their offence. The resulting struggle was long and
bitter, neither side would yield an inch and appeals to the
Pope, excommunications and vindictive fines were the
order of the day. At one moment Becket fled to Rome,
only to return a year or two later stimulated, refreshed
and eager for a renewal of the dispute. Finally, Henry
lost his temper and in a moment of rashness, while staying
in Normandy, expressed a wish that he might once and
for all be rid of " this turbulent priest." Unluckily four
of his companions took him at his word and immediately
crossed over to England, where they dispatched the
Archbishop on the steps of his own altar. Cordially
as the King had come to detest his Primate, when the
news of the tragedy reached him Henry was stricken

with remorse and immediately embarked on a series of extensive and rigorous penances.

Henry's last years were rendered unhappy not only by a guilty conscience but also by the unfilial behaviour of his sons. These four mediæval gangsters, aided and abetted by their mother, whose vigorous independence the advancing years had in no way diminished, were constantly intriguing against their father and with the assistance of his chief enemy, the King of France, succeeded on several occasions in organizing widespread rebellion. His two elder sons, Henry and Geoffrey, had frequently caused their father trouble in the past, and Henry had accustomed himself to regard them as potential enemies ; what broke his spirit was the discovery that Richard was equally treacherous. Finally, in 1189, when Richard whom he had constantly pardoned was once more in revolt and Henry learnt that on this occasion his youngest and best-loved child John was also on the rebels' side, he was so overcome by grief that he there and then granted all his sons' demands and died broken-hearted a few weeks later.

Although Henry's gifts of organization and leadership were of inestimable benefit to England it would be a mistake to reckon him one of our national heroes, for by birth and education he was a foreigner and singularly little of his time was spent in this country, which he regarded as merely an outlying part, although an extremely important one, of his great empire. The fact that his interests and the greater part of his possessions lay on the continent was highly advantageous for England as had Henry not possessed ample external resources and had he been forced to rely entirely on the support of his English subjects, he could never have succeeded in restoring the royal authority as thoroughly and as quickly as he did.

RICHARD I (Cœur de Lion)
1189 1199

From his tomb at Fontevrault

RICHARD I 1189—1199

RICHARD, who now succeeded his father on the throne of England, was a strikingly handsome man of thirty-two whose life for the past fifteen years had been chiefly spent in vexing the patience of his father and emulating the gallantry of his mother, both of which pastimes he had found highly congenial. Fully conscious of the splendour of his new position and naturally prone to *folie de la grandeur* his first concern on becoming king was to distinguish himself by some notable and magnificent exploit of arms. Luckily for him a splendid opportunity soon presented itself in the shape of the Third Crusade, and immediately after his coronation, a ceremony of unexampled magnificence that was only slightly marred by a severe outbreak of Jew-baiting in which the majority of the non-Aryan inhabitants of London perished, Richard set about collecting the necessary funds for equipping what proved to be one of the most fantastic military expeditions which ever set sail from Europe. In 1190, having raised every penny he could by the sale of offices, the mortgaging of the Crown Lands and numerous loans, he arrived in Sicily, at the head of an enormous armament, where he joined forces with the King of France. At first these two paladins were on the best of terms, but when Richard, whose patience was always sorely tried by any prolonged interval of peace, started a private war with King Tancred of Sicily, their relations became strained ; nor were matters improved by Richard's marriage in the following year to Berengaria of Navarre, despite the fact that he had been for a long time formally betrothed to the French King's sister.

However, Philip of France was not the only prince among the Crusaders whose enmity Richard soon succeeded in provoking. When the King of England at length arrived at Acre, having stopped *en route* in order to prosecute a small private war against the King of Cyprus, he lost no time in insulting and permanently antagonizing both the Duke of Austria and the Count of Montferrat. At the siege of Ascalon he went even further and, adding injury to insult, actually kicked the former in public, an action he was subsequently to regret. Shortly after the arrival of the Crusade in the Holy Land, Philip of France was forced to return home and left the command of the French troops in the hands of the Duke of Burgundy, with whom Richard was soon on the worst possible terms.

In the intervals when they were not quarrelling among themselves the Crusaders fought several engagements with the Infidels, in all of which Richard was conspicuous for his gallantry ; but the campaign as a whole hung fire, and by the end of the year the Christian army was still a long way from Jerusalem. In the following spring Richard received news that his brother John, who contrary to orders had installed himself in England, was behaving in a highly autocratic and presumptuous manner and that the King's return was ardently desired. On receipt of this information Richard made a treaty with Saladin and prepared to return to Europe, where the majority of his companions-in-arms had already gone.

Owing to his former behaviour he was unable to return by way of Sicily, and his unfortunate differences of opinion with the King of France made any journey through that country hazardous in the extreme, so he therefore decided to go back by way of central Europe. The first part of his journey ended when he was ship-wrecked on the Dalmatian coast, whence he was forced to continue his travels in disguise. He got as far as the neighbourhood of Vienna in safety, but there he was recognized and promptly imprisoned by the Duke of Austria, for whom the memory of the kick still rankled. At first Richard's predicament was known only to the Emperor, the King of France and John, none of whom had any interest in his release, but eventually the news reached Queen Eleanor, who immediately set about her son's rescue with all her customary energy. At last Richard's whereabouts was discovered, it is said, by a troubadour, who recognized his master's voice singing in his lofty cell. Thereupon, after protracted negotiations and the payment of a large ransom, to which all England with the exception of John willingly subscribed, Richard was at length able to return to his kingdom, in which he had not set foot for four years.

Richard remained among the subjects to whom he had been at last so happily restored for just so long as it took him to collect the necessary arms and money to embark on a war with his old enemy the King of France.

In 1199, after five years' desultory warfare, when his constitution had become seriously impaired by the hardships which he had undergone and the debauchery in which latterly he had constantly indulged, Richard was wounded by a poisoned arrow and died after a short illness.

Richard Cœur de Lion, despite the fact that he was by far the most celebrated prince of his day and that his memory was subsequently reverenced by many generations of his subjects, did little by his rule to benefit his kingdom. Even more of a foreigner than his father, never being able to speak a word of English, he regarded this country chiefly as a source from which he could obtain the necessary funds and men to embark on his career of glory. However, if he was more interested in increasing his own reputation than in safeguarding his country's welfare, his rule was nevertheless just and firm, and in the years that immediately followed his death his subjects came to realize that an absentee hero was infinitely preferable to a stay-at-home tyrant.

JOHN
1199-1216

From his tomb in Worcester Cathedral

THE character of John, who now succeeded his brother, was compound in equal degrees of vice, unscrupulousness and hopeless inefficiency : in addition to his father's pride, his brothers' cruelty and his mother's lack of moral balance he displayed a quality of pointless treachery that was all his own. At the time of his accession there existed another and possibly more legitimate candidate to the throne in the person of his late brother Geoffrey's son, Arthur of Brittany, and the cause of this young prince was supported by the King of·France and many of John's continental vassals. In the war which ensued, the aged and indomitable Eleanor of Aquitaine was besieged in her castle of Mirabel in Poitou by Arthur and Hugh de Lusignan, whose fiancée, Isabella of Angoulême, John had carried off after he had succeeded in obtaining a divorce of dubious legality from his first wife. Acting, for almost the only time in his life, with promptitude and decision, John marched to his mother's rescue and succeeded in capturing the person of his rival, and in a few months' time the unfortunate Arthur had been murdered by his unnatural uncle in person. However, John was quite incapable of any prolonged display of energy, and having settled the question of the succession in this drastic and definite manner, he now devoted himself to the pleasures of the table and the bed while his continental dominions were

being overrun by his enemies. A short while later
occurred the death of the aged Queen Eleanor, from
whose energy and enormous political experience her
sons had always derived the greatest advantage. Now
that she was dead the last chance of John's achieving the
smallest measure of success as a ruler had vanished.

Having lost the whole of his continental possessions
with the exception of Gascony and Aquitaine, John
returned to England, where he was soon involved in a
bitter and protracted quarrel with the Papacy. Pope
Innocent III, a strong-minded and autocratic prelate, had
appointed as Archbishop of Canterbury Stephen Langton
in preference both to the King's and to the cathedral
chapter's candidates. His choice was admirable, but his
high-handed methods quite justifiably provoked John's
furious indignation. Had the King been content to
take his stand purely on the question of the right of
appointment all might have been well, but he characteristically embarked on a policy of thoroughgoing and
unscrupulous anti-clericalism which soon lost him the
support of his subjects and brought the whole country
under an interdict. Finally, after a five-years' struggle
which had outraged the religious feeling of his people,
John was forced by Innocent's action in declaring him
deposed and his country forfeit to the King of France
to give way ; he did so in such a grovelling manner
and with such loss of dignity that he only succeeded in
alienating the loyalty of his subjects still further.

In 1214 John embarked on yet another disastrous campaign in France, and during his absence the enmity and

discontent of his barons, who had now found a leader in the person of the new Archbishop, formidably increased. On his return from abroad he found himself faced with a menacing combination of his most powerful subjects and after a few weeks of fruitless manœuvring he was forced to come to terms with them on the island of Runnymede. He was there presented with, and forced to sign, the celebrated document known as Magna Carta. Among the numerous rights which were therein enumerated, all of which John had at one time or other grossly infringed, the most important were those which reaffirmed the privilege of every man to be tried by a jury of his peers, forbade that any man should be tried twice for the same offence, and, most important of all, that which deprived the King of the ability to raise taxes without the consent of Parliament. These have ever since remained the foundations on which our constitution rests.

The fact that John had signed this charter was no indication that he had any intention of abiding by its provisions, and it was not long before he appealed to his old enemy the Pope to be released from his commitments and to be given his spiritual support in the inevitable struggle with the barons, who thereupon promptly appealed to Louis the Dauphin to come over and take the crown. After a year's civil war in which neither side gained any striking advantage, John, with his usual inefficiency, managed to lose all his baggage, including the crown of England, while crossing the Wash, and the chagrin which this caused him, combined with the drastic effects of a bout of gross overeating to carry him off a few weeks later.

Of all our kings John had probably the least to recommend him. As cruel as Richard III, as lecherous as Henry VIII, as untrustworthy as Charles I, and as ineffectual as Stephen, his sole redeeming feature seems to have been that, like so many celebrated criminals, he was invariably kind to his mother.

HENRY III
1216-1272

From his tomb in Westminster Abbey

HENRY III 1216—1272

THE career of Henry III provides an admirable example of the occasional operation of a law which determines the survival of the unfittest. In an age when the weakest were apt to go to the wall with almost monotonous regularity he somehow contrived, although deficient in all the qualities which constitute leadership, to misgovern his kingdom for a longer period than any sovereign before George III and yet to escape the usual disastrous consequences of royal folly too long prolonged. Had his private life been a quarter as disgraceful as his notorious father's he would not have retained his throne for five years, but luckily he was a chaste and upright man whose piety and goodwill were generally recognized even when his extravagance and hopeless muddle-headedness had become all too familiar to his long-suffering subjects.

At the time of his accession Henry was still a youth and the government of the country remained in the hands of William the Marshal, the best of John's advisers, the Justiciar Hubert de Burgh and Archbishop Langton, until 1227, when the King declared himself of fit age to govern. For many years there had been grumblings at the excessive influence of foreigners, either priests or powerful mercenaries whom the late King had brought over from France and had subsequently remained here, and when Langton died in the same year, de Burgh remained almost the sole Englishman in a position of authority. The young King now rapidly showed himself only too eager to assist this foreign invasion; his excessive piety led him to welcome the arrival of innumerable prelates from Rome and his marriage in 1236 to Eleanor of Provence heralded the coming of droves of impoverished Provençal in-laws, all of whom had to be accommodated in lucrative positions. In 1232 Henry dismissed his faithful adviser de Burgh and appointed in his place the Bishop of Winchester, one of his father's old French protégés. So much resentment did this cause that in less than two years Henry was forced to get rid of the Bishop and thereupon reached the unfortunate decision to abolish both the office of Justiciar and of Chancellor and from henceforth to govern the land himself.

The history of the next twenty-four years amply proves that few men have been less fitted to undertake the arduous business of government than Henry. By allowing the Papal Legate to exact enormous sums from the Church, by engaging in a futile and disastrous war with France and by constantly acceding to his blood-sucking relatives' endless demands for money he succeeded in bringing his country to the very brink of bankruptcy. At last in 1258 he overreached himself in folly. Having pledged England's credit to the Pope to the extent of 140,000 marks, in return for the very dubious reward of a reversion on the Crown of Sicily, he had the effrontery to summon Parliament, who had never been consulted in the matter at all, and request them to pay up. The result was a sudden outburst of popular

indignation for which anyone less simple-minded than
the King would have been prepared. The disgruntled
barons had at last found a leader and a mouthpiece in
Simon de Montfort, a nobleman of foreign origin and
brother-in-law to the King, who had become in the
course of a long career in this country more English
than the English, and Henry now found himself forced
to submit all his decrees to three committees appointed
by Parliament and strictly to abide by the provisions of
Magna Carta, many of which he had long grown
accustomed to disregard. However, his good behaviour
was not of long duration and four years later he came to
blows with the popular party of Simon de Montfort.
Each side had a considerable armed following and the
opposing forces met beneath the walls of Lewes. In the
ensuing battle the King's forces were completely defeated,
largely owing to the rashness of Henry's eldest son
Edward, and the King himself fell into the hands of his
enemies.

For the next two years the country was governed
in fact if not in name by de Montfort, whose most
notable act was the summoning of the Parliament of
1265. This was the first Parliament in the modern
sense of the word ever to be called together in England ;
in it were included not only the barons, the Church
dignitaries and the shire Knights but also representatives
from the towns. It would, however, be a mistake to
assume that Montfort was particularly eager to further
democratic ideals, for he merely included the members
from the charter boroughs, on whom the King's illegal

taxes had placed the heaviest burden, in order to assure himself of the requisite majority. Just and equitable as was his rule, Earl Simon soon antagonized a large number of his fellow-barons, and when in 1266 Henry's son Edward succeeded in escaping from the honourable confinement in which he had recently been kept, that intrepid young man experienced no difficulty in collecting a large body of supporters. With these he attacked and completely defeated the forces of Simon de Montfort at the battle of Evesham, in which the great earl himself lost his life.

For the rest of his reign, Henry, who was now restored to the full exercise of his royal functions, governed with discretion and moderation. He had, at long last, learnt his lesson and died in his bed in 1272 : a peaceful end which no one would have predicted for so wayward and incompetent a monarch.

EDWARD I
1272-1307

*From a XIVth Century MSS.
in the British Museum*

EDWARD I 1272—1307

AT the time of Henry III's death his eldest son Edward was absent on the Sixth Crusade, and there is no more striking proof of the tranquillity which the kingdom now enjoyed than that provided by the fact that the new King did not consider it necessary to hurry home at once and only arrived in his kingdom some eighteen months after his actual accession.

Edward I was a complete contrast to his father in almost every way : efficient, thrifty and just, the only thing he had in common with the late King was a private life of unblemished virtue.

His first action on his return was to engage in a campaign against the Welsh, who had long been accustomed to ravage the Marches, as the border districts were called, at the first suitable opportunity. In the course of two campaigns, 1275 and 1282, Edward completely reduced the whole country and put an end to this menace once and for all. During the next few years Edward devoted himself to legislation with as much success as he had done to warfare and there now appeared on the statute book a series of excellent laws : *De Religiosis*, which was intended to prevent the accumulation of enormous estates in the hands of the Church; *De Donis*, which forbade landholders to alienate their property from their heirs *Quia*; *Emptores*, which modified the feudal system so as to favour the Crown at the expense of the great barons, and finally the Statute of Winchester, which reorganized the national militia. So great a reputation as a legislator did Edward soon enjoy that in 1292 he was asked to arbitrate in a dispute between two rival claimants to the throne of Scotland. His decision was just, and generally accepted, but was to prove productive of much trouble in the next few years.

In 1294 Edward became involved in a bitter quarrel with the King of France who, by a piece of barefaced treachery, had got possession of several important border castles in Edward's French possessions and both monarchs were preparing for war. At this juncture, Balliol, King of Scotland, who owed his throne to Edward's good offices, took the opportunity of stabbing his benefactor in the back and threw in his lot with the French. Edward at once abandoned for the moment his proposed campaign on the continent and marched north to deal with the treacherous Scots, whom he experienced no difficulty in defeating. Having captured all their principal strongholds he deposed the wretched Balliol, put the kingdom in charge of one of his own lieutenants and returned to England with all the Scottish Crown Jewels, including the historic stone of Scone, in his baggage. He now proposed to resume his interrupted conflict with France, but almost at once encountered considerable opposition from his own barons, who were not overeager for the fray and maintained that their feudal obligations did not compel them to serve save under the immediate command of the King himself. Thus Edward's plan for dividing his forces into two separate armies acting simultaneously on different fronts proved impractical, owing to his inability to be in two places at once, and he was forced to confine his operations to Northern France, where he failed to gain any conspicuous success and whence he was compelled to return home in 1297 on receipt of bad news from the North.

The Scots were once more up in arms and this time they had, in the person of William Wallace, a far more capable leader than Balliol. Although Edward completely annihilated the Scottish forces at the battle of Falkirk it was not until 1305, by which time he had patched up a truce with the French, that he finally succeeded in subduing the whole country. Peace, however, was not of long duration, and in 1306 the place of Wallace, whom Edward had captured and hanged, was taken by Robert Bruce, who was almost at once defeated by an English force under the Earl of Pembroke but just managed to escape with his life and returned in the following year to renew the struggle. Edward was by now a very old man, but nevertheless he determined once more to return to Scotland and personally to undertake the final chastisement of that troublesome land. He got as far as Carlisle, but there his strength failed him and he died before he could cross the Border.

Edward I, by his legislative ability, the firm control he exercised over his barons and the constant attention which he paid to the welfare of his people, accomplished more for his country's greatness than any other of our mediæval Kings. Severe but just, he showed himself merciful to all save traitors and Jews : for the financial activities of the latter he entertained a profound and, it must be admitted, quite justifiable mistrust, and in 1290 he expelled them all. Although a good fighting man he was without any overwhelming military genius and in the course of his career he probably lost as many battles as he gained, but his victories were always more important than his defeats, and it was he who first realized the importance of the longbow, a weapon which was later to render our armies almost invincible.

EDWARD II
1307-1327

From a drawing by Professor E. W. Tristram
of a wall painting in Westminster Abbey

EDWARD II 1307—1327

THE last wish that Edward I had expressed had been that the campaign against Scotland, which had brought about his death, should be continued by his son. It would appear that illness and old age had seriously affected the usually shrewd judgment of the old King, for if he seriously considered that there was any likelihood of his wishes being fulfilled his opinion of his heir was undoubtedly coloured by a quite unjustified optimism. So far the first Prince of Wales had given no evidence of any very marked qualities other than a rather suspicious fondness for the company of his social inferiors that it would be foolish to regard as any indication of a welcome sympathy for the ideals of democracy. Now that his father was dead, Edward II showed no inclination to undergo the hardships and dangers of a protracted and arduous war and immediately hurried back to London to make the final arrangements for his forthcoming marriage with Isabella of France, and only returned to the north in order to bring the campaign to a speedy and ignominious conclusion.

The atmosphere of the new King's court was soon heavy with suspicion and jealousy. While Edward was still a boy his father had, in a rash moment, provided him with a playmate of his own age but inferior station named Piers Gaveston, to whom the young prince had rapidly become violently attached. This friendship had never become stale and now the King loaded his old friend with riches and honours. The natural resentment which this caused among the older nobility was in no way lessened by the behaviour of Gaveston himself, an ostentatious and malicious young man who took every opportunity of exercising what seems to have been a rather adolescent sense of humour at the expense of the more respected members of the King's household. Again and again the barons, led by the King's cousin, Thomas of Lancaster, brought pressure to bear on their infatuated sovereign and succeeded in obtaining the exile of the detested favourite, but each time he was recalled and reinstated in all his positions after an all too short absence abroad. At last in 1312, on one of the few occasions when he was not in the company of the King, Gaveston was caught by Lancaster, who forthwith beheaded him beside the public highway.

With the death of Gaveston Edward recovered some of his popularity, but he did not long retain it, for two years later he embarked on a campaign against the Scots which culminated in the total defeat of the English forces at the battle of Bannockburn. For the next six years the administration was carried on largely by Lancaster, who despite a great parade of energy soon proved himself quite as incompetent as the King. The Scotch war still dragged on, and the lack of success which attended the English arms did much to diminish Lancaster's shaky prestige. Meanwhile Edward had found others to take Gaveston's place, and the reigning favourites were now the Despencers, father and son. In 1321 Lancaster succeeded in securing their banishment and once more felt reasonably secure. However, he had made the grave mistake of underestimating his sovereign, who under a cloak of natural indolence concealed not only a long memory but considerable firmness of purpose. Edward now suddenly exerted himself and seized the two Mortimers, Lancaster's chief supporters, and sent them to the Tower. The next year he captured Lancaster himself who had fled to the North, and that nobleman was then dispatched with as little ceremony as had attended the execution of Gaveston ten years before. Edward's mind, like the mills of God, worked slowly, but its operations were similarly effective.

However, Edward was not the only person who could nurse a grievance. Queen Isabella, a young and beautiful woman, had long been jealous of her husband's favourites and resentful of the neglect with which she was treated, and in 1325 she departed to Paris, where she was joined by Roger Mortimer, who the previous year had escaped from the Tower, probably with her assistance. She now started to intrigue against her husband, whose new favourites, the Despencers, were as cordially disliked as Gaveston had been. In 1326, in rather premature widow's weeds, she landed in Suffolk with a considerable force and marched against the King, who had fled to Gloucester. On the way she caught and hanged the elder Despencer at Bristol and soon after Edward himself was handed over to her by the Welsh, with whom he had taken refuge. At first he was kept in an honourable confinement, but gradually his treatment deteriorated, and finally in 1327 he was assassinated in a most barbarous and ingenious fashion.

Edward II was an indolent and rather pathetic figure who had been neglected in childhood and as a result was far too easily influenced by the worthless company that he displayed an uncanny skill in selecting. Had he been born in a more settled age he would most likely have died in his bed after a reign in which it is improbable that he would have accomplished very much either for good or evil. As to his morals, much is suspected but little known. However, to presume, as some have done, that his moral code was high, on the evidence of his reported remark that after first seeing his wife he found himself unable to like another woman, is to overlook a certain ambiguity inherent in that rather improbable utterance.

EDWARD III
1327-1377

*From a XIVth Century MSS.
in the British Museum*

EDWARD III 1327—1377

QUEEN ELEANOR had brought with her from France her son Edward, a precocious youth of fourteen who, on the deposition of his father, was proclaimed king. For the first three years of the new reign the government was carried on by the Queen and Roger Mortimer, whom Isabella had discovered to be a far more satisfactory companion than her late husband. Their rule was extravagant, tyrannical and inefficient, and they were soon on bad terms with a number of the barons. In 1330 the young King took matters into his own hands and with a small body of friends surprised his mother and her lover at Nottingham castle : the former he confined to a castle in Norfolk, the latter he hanged at Tyburn, and from now on he ruled his kingdom for himself.

The first enterprise on which Edward embarked after his assumption of power was a war with Scotland which, despite a great victory for his arms at Halidon Hill in 1333, he failed to bring to any decisive conclusion. His reason for abandoning this campaign half-way through was that in the year 1337 he was presented with an admirable excuse for starting a far more spectacular war in France. In 1328 the King of that country, Edward's own uncle, had died without leaving an heir to succeed him. The crown had then passed to his cousin Philip of Valois by reason of the Salic Law which decreed that the crown could only descend through the male line. Edward, who was admittedly a closer relative of the late King than Philip, maintained that the Salic Law was so much nonsense and that the crown of France was his by right of succession, and now the outbreak of some purely local hostilities on the borders of Gascony provided him with the opportunity for which he had been waiting to support his claims by force of arms. Raising every penny he could lay his hands on, Edward crossed to France at the head of a large army and that disastrous conflict, the Hundred Years War, had begun. For the first few years the struggle proved unsuccessful and extremely expensive for the English, and Edward's only success was a great naval victory at Sluys. However, in 1346 the fortunes of war changed and, having successfully ravaged Normandy for several months, Edward met and totally defeated a French army many times larger than his own at the battle of Crécy. A year later he captured the vitally important town of Calais after a protracted siege which so exhausted his patience that the principal citizens owed their lives to the good offices of his wife, Queen Phillipa, an intelligent and soft-hearted woman. Glorious as were these victories their effects were eclipsed in the following year by a fearful disaster which involved the whole of Europe. There broke out a terrible and mysterious pestilence which, starting in Asia, spread westwards with terrifying rapidity. Everywhere the population was shockingly reduced and the consequent dislocation of economic life was both widespread and prolonged. How disastrous were the effects of this plague may be gauged by the fact that the French and English were forced to curb their insatiable bellicosity for the space of seven years, and it was not until 1355 that either side found itself in a position to renew hostilities.

This new campaign was conducted not by Edward himself, who was busy ravaging Scotland, but by his eldest son the celebrated Black Prince who had already proved himself as redoubtable a fighting man as his father. From his base at Bordeaux the Prince carried hostilities into the heart of the enemy's country and in 1356 he won the great victory of Poictiers, where the French were once more completely defeated and their King himself taken prisoner. The war dragged on for another four years; but the loss of their King had completely disorganized the enemy, and in 1360 they were forced to conclude a most unfavourable peace by the Treaty of Bretigny, and Edward now regained all those territories which had been lost by the incompetence of John and Henry III. However, England derived little ultimate benefit from this long-drawn-out warfare, for the expenses had been enormous and it was not long before many of the newly acquired territories were in open revolt. In a short time the Black Prince was involved in a futile dynastic struggle in Spain from which he returned with a lingering disease which undermined his constitution and finally killed him.

The last years of Edward III were far from happy. Everywhere the majestic fabric of the mediæval structure was beginning to crack; the gross materialism and absence of all spiritual values observable in many of the higher ecclesiastics caused widespread discontent and the Church was rent by schism; the economic conditions occasioned by the results of the Black Death were responsible for putting strange new ideas into the heads of the lower classes; the ideals of chivalry were rapidly degenerating into excuses for indiscriminate blood-letting and privileged oppression. Edward himself in his old age provides an admirable symbol of the changing conditions of the times. Always precocious (he had been a father at seventeen) he was now prematurely enfeebled and his youthful passions had deteriorated into a senile and insatiable lust, his high courage into mere bravado and bloodthirstiness. He who had ruled his people with so firm a hand was now incapable of maintaining order in his own household. In his declining years he displayed something of his father's fondness for low company and when he died in 1377, miserable and deserted, the body of this once mighty prince was stripped of its jewellery and its rings by women of the humblest origin and the lowest morals who had latterly been his sole companions.

RICHARD II
1377-1399

*From the painting in the National
Portrait Gallery*

RICHARD II 1377—1399

RICHARD, a boy of ten, who now succeeded his grandfather, was the only surviving son of the Black Prince. At the beginning of his reign he laboured under the disadvantage of having too many and too powerful uncles, an embarrassment from which several subsequent monarchs were also to suffer. During the last few years of the previous reign the government had been largely carried on by the eldest and most powerful of these, John of Gaunt, Duke of Lancaster, who, although he had inherited a fair measure of his father's ability, had succeeded, by his proneness to engage in expensive and unnecessary foreign expeditions and the tolerance which he extended to the reforming party in the Church, in antagonizing a large section of popular opinion, and as a result his unfortunate nephew found himself faced by a no means promising situation. Richard had not been on the throne four years when a dangerous and unusual revolt of the peasantry broke out and so successful did it prove that in a short time the capital was threatened by an enormous band of armed and infuriated labourers. In this crisis the young King behaved with great coolness and judgment and by his presence of mind in riding out and promising the rebels that their grievances should be remedied averted an imminent catastrophe. The popularity which this action gained him was far from welcome to Lancaster, and uncle and nephew were soon on bad terms. Richard, who had been married to Anne of Bohemia in 1383, had by now made friends of his own whom he promoted to various positions in the Government, and Lancaster left England to engage in yet another of his unsuccessful military adventures in Spain.

However, the departure of John of Gaunt did not, as Richard had hoped, provide him with the opportunity of doing what he liked and in 1387, after an unsuccessful attempt at a *coup d'état*, which resulted in the banishment of many of his friends, he found himself once more under the detested tutelage of his uncles. But these worthies soon proved themselves even more unfit to govern than the absent Lancaster and when in 1389 Richard made another, and this time successful, bid for power there was general satisfaction.

For the next five years all went well : the young King governed constitutionally with the assistance of Parliament, and although his personal extravagance gave rise to some criticism he retained much of his popularity. His uncle Lancaster, who had returned from Spain, was now on the best of terms with his nephew, to whom he gave the full benefit of his advice, founded on a long experience. But in 1394 Richard suffered a terrible bereavement ; his young wife, to whom he had been passionately devoted and who had always proved an admirable influence on her husband, suddenly died, and from henceforward Richard's character was strangely changed. He had always been an extravagant and splendour-loving prince, but he now indulged in a perpetual orgy of fantastic expenditure and ostentatious display. Moreover, he became increasingly inclined to assume autocratic powers and to dispense with the services of Parliament. In 1397 he suddenly arrested his uncle Gloucester together with the Earls of Arundel and Warwick. Warwick was exiled, Arundel beheaded and Gloucester died in prison with a mysterious but convenient suddenness. In the following year he banished his cousin Nottingham and John of Gaunt's son Henry of Lancaster, and on the death of the latter's father he confiscated the whole of his enormous inheritance. He then suddenly departed on a necessary but inopportune expedition to Ireland, leaving the government of the kingdom in the hands of the Duke of York, the most amiable and least competent of his uncles. The King had not long arrived in Ireland when Henry of Lancaster landed in Yorkshire, where he was soon joined by large numbers of the nobility whom the perpetual extravagance and erratic conduct of the absent King had led to desert his cause. Richard at once returned to England, but owing to a series of accidents and his own mismanagement he soon found himself without support and was forced to surrender to the Archbishop of Canterbury and Earl Percy at Conway, to whom he made a formal offer of abdication. This was subsequently confirmed on his arrival in London and from now on his days were numbered. The exact circumstances and date of his death are obscure, but to presume that it was the result of natural causes would be to credit Henry of Lancaster with an unusual and improbable clemency.

Unfortunate, intelligent and artistic, Richard II is a strangely sympathetic and individual figure. A great patron of the arts, his love of splendour and magnificence, though common among continental monarchs, is only paralleled in English history by Henry VIII and George IV. The happiness of his domestic life was almost equally unusual, and it is charitable and probable to suppose that his extraordinary conduct during his later years was in a large measure the result of a sudden overwhelming shock upon a temperament that was always nervous and highly strung. As the fourteenth century drew to a close the shadows of approaching gloom were beginning to deepen all over Europe, and it is fitting that its end should have coincided with that of Richard, whose life and character foreshadowed in so many ways the end of the Middle Ages.

HENRY IV
1399-1413

From a painting in the National Portrait Gallery

HENRY IV 1399—1413

ON the abdication of Richard II in 1399, Parliament, disregarding the fact that by the strict laws of inheritance the young Earl of March, a great-grandson of Edward III's second son, had a prior claim, declared Henry of Lancaster King, and he was crowned late in the same year. At the time of his accession he was thirty-two years of age and a man of keen judgment and wide experience. Although he was the first English king to have been born in England of English parents, he had travelled extensively and subsequently retained an international outlook unusual among recent sovereigns whose vision had all too frequently been bounded by France. In his youth he had fought in a crusade with the Teutonic Knights in Prussia, had visited the Kings of Hungary and Bohemia and the Doge of Venice and had also been on a pilgrimage to the Holy Land. His time of exile he had spent at Paris.

At the beginning of his reign his position, though strong, was by no means unassailable, and in order to render it secure he was forced to make concessions that he regretted and to take drastic steps which frequently went against his religious scruples. It is probable that he considered his cousin's death an unavoidable necessity which he did not for a moment shrink from compassing, but it is unlikely that his conscience was ever again entirely clear. Being a religious man he was now

doubly anxious for the Church's approval, and in order
to obtain it readily acquiesced in their fierce persecution
of the Lollards and other heretics, and his reign has the
unenviable distinction of being the one in which the
law " De Heretico Comburendo " first appeared on the
statute book and the first in which a heretic was ever
burnt in England. Although by these and similar concessions to religious prejudice he succeeded in gaining
the support of the Church, the loyalty of the great
nobles by whose aid he had gained his crown soon
proved far more difficult to retain, and in 1403 he was
faced with a formidable revolt in the North, led his
former allies the Percies and assisted by the Welsh, with
whom the late King had always been popular. This he
was successful in crushing at the battle of Shrewsbury
but was nevertheless forced to undertake a further campaign against the Welsh the next year. In 1405 another
rebellion broke out in the North, and although he suppressed it without much difficulty he was compelled to
execute the Archbishop of York, an act which troubled
still further a conscience that was already overburdened.

The strain and worry of these events now began
seriously to affect the King's health and for the remainder
of his reign Henry was almost a complete invalid. He
had married as his second wife Joan of Navarre, and
his son by his first wife, Henry, afterwards Henry V,
was soon on bad terms with his stepmother, which made
his relations with his father, who rightly or wrongly
suspected him of concealing an unfilial impatience to
succeed, exceptionally painful and difficult. At last in

1413, worn out by the responsibilities which he had been so eager to assume, Henry collapsed and died while at his devotions in Westminster Abbey, hvaing suffered for the last five years from a disease the symptoms of which were horrible in the extreme and the nature probably some type of leprosy.

Henry IV was a practical, unimaginative man who, owing to the fact that he was indebted for his title to the throne not to the laws of succession but the elective powers vested in Parliament, was forced, whether he wished it or not, to be a strictly constitutional monarch. He shared none of his predecessor's artistic tastes but was nevertheless well educated and intelligent : he patronized Chaucer and Gower and corresponded with a wide range of foreign sovereigns, including the Byzantine Emperor, who actually paid him what proved to be an extremely expensive visit early in his reign, and that exceedingly remote figure the Emperor of Abyssinia : the first but not, alas, the last appearance of that potentate in our history.

Sandwiched between two such colourful, although such different figures as Richard II and Henry V, Henry IV tends to appear rather drab and commonplace, but the immediate past had shown and the future was to reinforce the lesson that for a king there are many more dangerous and less welcome qualities than drabness, and for a monarch to be commonplace is to share a characteristic widely distributed among his subjects.

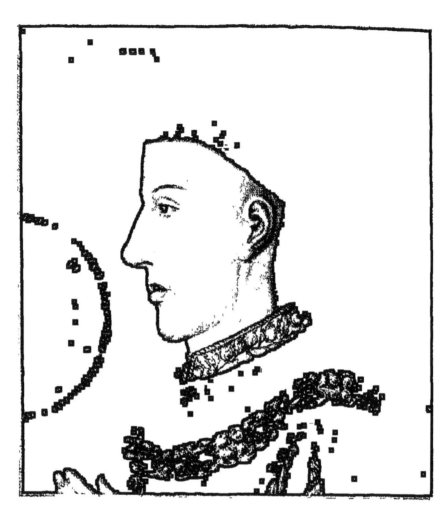

HENRY V
1413-1422

From a painting in the National Portrait Gallery

HENRY V 1413—1422

AROUND few of our sovereigns have so many legends been woven with so few facts to substantiate them as around the figure of Henry V as a young man. He is familiarly pictured as a dashing young rakehell whom the ceremony of his coronation recalled to a sense of his responsibilities with all the suddenness of an evangelical conversion. As, in point of fact, most of his time as Prince of Wales was spent on the Welsh border where he fulfilled the arduous duties of Regent and keeper of the peace with an efficiency that was universally acknowledged by his contemporaries, his acquaintance with the night life of the capital must necessarily have been slight and occasional. However, of his rectitude and piety as king no shadow of doubt exists and the fact remains that he himself was accustomed to regard his former life as something of which to be deeply ashamed ; probably with as little justification as the average convert who labours under a deep, and usually erroneous sense of guilt, for there was undoubtedly a marked revivalist strain in his character.

A bellicose young man, ardently desirous of military glory, Henry's first action after succeeding was to revive his great-grandfather's claims on the French Throne. In so doing he was not entirely actuated by a personal longing for renown, for he was well aware that a successful foreign campaign would do much to strengthen both the Crown and his own rather dubious title to it and, moreover, his nobles were longing for a war which the distracted internal condition of France seemed to indicate would not prove difficult to bring to a successful and speedy conclusion. Accordingly when in 1414 his demands for the return of Normandy, Anjou, Maine and Touraine together with the hand of the Princess Katherine were refused by the French Dauphin, Henry immediately began to prepare for war.

In 1415 Henry landed in France with an enormous army and laid siege to Harfleur. After six weeks the town surrendered, but the English had in the meantime suffered severely from disease and it was with a greatly reduced force that Henry set off across country to Calais. The French with a vastly larger army at once hurried to cut him off and the two armies met at Agincourt. In the battle which followed the English were completely victorious ; the casualties suffered by the French were enormous and included the Constable of France himself and the flower of the French nobility. On his return to England, Henry found that the news of this great victory had enormously strengthened his position and Parliament now made no difficulty about granting him further supplies with which to renew the campaign in the following year.

The war of 1417–1420 was even more successful and by the terms of the treaty which brought it to a close, Henry's claims were fully recognized, he was given the

Princess Katherine as wife and was made Regent of France for the lifetime of Charles VI with the succession to the throne on the death of that aged and imbecile monarch. After making a state entry into Paris he left his brother Clarence behind to guard his interests and returned with his bride to London. However, he did not long remain in his native country, for in 1421 news was brought him that his brother had been defeated and killed by the forces of the Dauphin, and Henry was forced once more to return to France. Having obtained, although not without difficulty, fresh grants from his loyal but war-weary Parliament, he set out with an army and succeeded in driving the Dauphin back over the Loire. Unfortunately Henry's constitution was no better equipped than his father's to stand the strain of continuous and prolonged campaigning, and now his health began rapidly to fail. In the following year he died at Paris aged thirty-five, having reigned a shorter time than any king since the Conquest.

Brave, generous and handsome, with a real genius for war, Henry V was generally regarded by his contemporaries as the noblest figure of his day and by posterity as the very pattern of chivalry. Unfortunately the virtues which he so abundantly displayed were not those of which a contemporary monarch stood most in need, and it may be doubted whether either England or Europe derived much benefit from the glorious victories of this thirteenth-century figure operating in the fifteenth. Moreover, there was a sanctimonious tinge about his celebrated piety, and it should not be forgotten that this perfect gentle knight was also one of the most relentless religious persecutors of the time. No other English monarch, with the exception of Mary, dealt so harshly with the unorthodox.

HENRY VI
1422-1461

From a painting in the National
Portrait Gallery

HENRY VI 1422—1461

ON the death of Henry V his son and heir was less than a year old and never before had the kingdom been faced with the prospect of so long a minority. Contrary to custom, the period when the government was in the hands of regents was the happiest part of Henry VI's reign, for his uncle the Duke of Bedford and his great-uncle the Cardinal Beaufort were capable and energetic, and both in England and France guarded the interests of their young sovereign in a careful and praiseworthy manner. The only difficulties which arose at this time came from the feather-brained behaviour of Humphrey, Duke of Gloucester, a younger brother of Henry V whom that monarch had made regent of England, considering that the Regency of France was a task more suited to the greater abilities of his brother Bedford.

At first the war in France proved as successful as it had done under the late King, but in 1429 the appearance of that strange and romantic figure, Joan of Arc, put new spirit into the hearts of the war-weary French and their apathetic Dauphin, and from that moment the English were dogged by misfortune. In 1431, when most of Henry V's conquests had been lost, the Maid of Orleans fell into the hands of the Duke of Burgundy, England's greatest ally, without whose aid we would not have been able to maintain our position in France for six months, who handed her over to the Duke of

Bedford. After a trial for witchcraft before the Bishop of Beauvais, at which edifying spectacle the infant King made one of his first public appearances, she was burnt at the stake in the market-place of Rouen. However, despite the elimination of Joan of Arc and the coronation of Henry VI as King of France in Notre-Dame, which took place a few weeks later, the war continued to go badly for the English, and on the death of Bedford and the defection of Burgundy their cause was lost: a fact which Gloucester and a strong war party in England refused to recognize and the hostilities dragged miserably on.

In 1444 a temporary truce was arranged and King Henry married Margaret of Anjou, a daughter of the titular King of Sicily and a kinswoman of the King of France. However, this interval of peace was far from welcome to Gloucester and Richard, Duke of York (a descendant through his mother of that Earl of Mortimer whose prior claim to the throne had been overlooked by Henry IV), who had shown himself a capable general and governor in Normandy, and from henceforth there were endless and bitter squabbles between their party and that of the Beauforts who had been largely responsible for the peace. In 1449 war broke out once more, and Normandy, which was now governed by Edmund Beaufort, Duke of Somerset, was soon lost to the French. This disaster rendered the party then in power so unpopular that Henry was forced by the pressure of public opinion to get rid of Suffolk, one of the Beauforts' principal supporters.

The next year there occurred a rising of the peasants in Kent and Sussex which was only suppressed with difficulty and gave the Duke of York the opportunity for which he had been waiting. He came over from Ireland where he had been in partial exile, and on the King's refusal to comply with his demands for the dismissal of Somerset he took up arms against his sovereign. At this juncture Henry's reason, which had never been strong, gave way completely, and York was unanimously elected Regent, thus gaining his ends without the necessity for a struggle. Unfortunately in less than eighteen months Henry had achieved the double feat of recovering his reason and becoming a father, and York's prospects were gloomier than ever, and when Somerset was taken from the Tower, where his rival had confined him and reinstated in his former position, the Duke realized that armed resistance was the only solution.

For the next fifteen years the country was rent by civil strife of appalling bitterness. Each side was composed of a large number of great nobles who welcomed the opportunity of paying off a variety of old personal scores and were enabled to continue the struggle indefinitely by reason of their great wealth and the vast supply of ex-servicemen left over from the French wars, who had retained a taste for warfare which they were only too eager to gratify. At first the Yorkists were successful, and at the battle of St. Albans captured the person of the King, who promptly went mad for the second time. For a while York resumed his former position, but the intrigues of the Queen, a determined and vindictive woman, soon brought about a renewal of the struggle which was continued with unabated ferocity. Sometimes the Yorkists were in the ascendant and sometimes the Lancastrians : sometimes the King was sane and sometimes he was mad. At length as a result of the great battle of Towton, the Lancastrians were completely defeated and a conflict in which all the principal protagonists, York, Somerset, the Percies and many more, had perished and which had witnessed the mutual extermination of half the aristocracy of England, finally came to end.

The Duke of York's eldest surviving son, Edward, now proclaimed himself king, and the unfortunate Henry fled to Scotland. In 1470 he returned once more to his unhappy throne as a result of an insurrection led by the great Earl of Warwick, formerly Edward's staunchest supporter, who had recently quarrelled with his master and had succeeded in driving him out of the country. However, the luckless Henry did not long enjoy his revived dignity, for in the following year Edward returned from abroad with a large army and completely defeated his faithless vassal at the battle of Barnet, and but a short time elapsed before the old King perished of that mysterious disease which so regularly carried off imprisoned monarchs in the Middle Ages and with which the fate of Richard II and Edward II has already rendered us familiar.

Henry VI was an amiable man whose weakness of character involved him in situations from which his saintly piety was incapable of extricating him and could only serve to enable him to bear his resulting misfortunes with fortitude and dignity. Cultured and well educated he displayed a great fondness for education and the arts, and Eton and King's College, Cambridge, are his most permanent memorials. For music he had a genuine aptitude and he enjoys the unique distinction of being the only monarch whose compositions have attained the posthumous dignity of a gramophone recording.

EDWARD IV
1461-1483

WHEN Edward IV was once more firmly re-estab-
lished on his throne he found himself in the
enviable position of being entirely free from enemies
and rivals : all who by their birth or position could
have challenged his authority had been eliminated in
the recent struggles. The sole remaining male descendant of John of Gaunt, other than the Kings of Spain
and Portugal, was Henry of Richmond, a son of Edmund
Tudor and Margaret Beaufort, who being a prudent
young man for his health's sake resided in Brittany.
Moreover, as the King had acquired the estates of all
his recently exterminated relations and had taken the
opportunity of confiscating those of their supporters, he
was in a position of financial independence and under
no necessity of ever summoning parliament unless he
was so inclined.

During his first period on the throne Edward had
married, much to the fury of the Earl of Warwick and
other of his partisans, Elizabeth Woodville, a beautiful
widow, his senior in years and his inferior by birth. By
her marriage this astute woman gained wealth and position not only for herself but also for her numerous
relatives, although she did not succeed in retaining for
long the affections of her exceedingly amorous husband.
In affairs of the heart Edward contrived to combine
business with pleasure in a novel and successful manner :

by choosing his mistresses from among the wives and daughters of the rich London merchants he not only increased his popularity in the City but also secured valuable financial support.

A similar acuteness characterized all Edward's actions which, combined with a complete absence of scruple, enabled him to make himself the most powerful and least trammelled monarch who had occupied the throne since the Angevins. In 1478, his brother the Duke of Clarence, a treacherous and foolish young man who had once before been discovered in treasonable practices, was so short-sighted as to renew his intrigues. When Edward got wind of what was happening he promptly dispatched his wretched brother to the Tower where he did not hesitate to have him secretly drowned in a butt of Malmsey wine, thus ensuring him an immortality which his life and character would never have secured. The methods he employed in dealing with potential enemies abroad, though less drastic, were far more profitable. From Louis IX of France he obtained, by the exertion of a little pressure at the right moment, a large sum of money and an annual pension, and the fact that this success involved a cynical betrayal of his old ally the Duke of Burgundy in no way troubled his cast-iron conscience. In a similar manner he tricked the Scotch King into a war at exactly the moment that was the most advantageous to himself and disastrous for the Scotch, and as a result recaptured the important town of Berwick.

Once the need for action had passed Edward relapsed

into a life of luxury and self-indulgence which did not, curiously enough, in any way impair either his judgment or his energy, and those who were foolish enough to presume his sloth and indolence had robbed him of his youthful fire sadly underestimated his ability to resume the rôle of man of action at a moment's notice. As a general his skill was enormous, and he never once lost a battle or assisted at a defeat. In his private life his devotion to the pleasures of the table was only equalled by his boundless concupiscence, and his love of display led him to adorn both his mistresses and his meals with trappings of unparalleled magnificence. His general ostentation and fondness for the society of wealthy merchants and others who had made a handsome profit out of the late hostilities did not, however, much impair his popularity save with the remnants of the old nobility, for as a great writer remarks, " Vulgarity in a king is flattering to the majority of his subjects."

Edward IV died in 1483 at the early age of forty-one, largely as a result of having consistently over-taxed his strength in his pursuit of pleasure. At his death he left behind him a numerous family and, a far more unusual accomplishment for an English King, no debts. Unscrupulous, avaricious and greedy, there was little in his life, either as a man or as king, to compel admiration save complete success.

EDWARD V
1483-1483

EDWARD V 1483—1483

EDWARD IV left two sons by his wife Elizabeth Woodville, Edward Prince of Wales, aged twelve, and Richard Duke of York, two years younger. At the time of his father's death the Prince of Wales was staying with his mother at Ludlow, and as the Queen and her relations were naturally not unapprehensive as to what course events would now take, they were careful to safeguard the interests of the new King in so far as lay in their power. Elizabeth's son by her first marriage, Lord Dorset, seized the royal treasure in the Tower, and it was only as a result of the most earnest entreaties on the part of the Council that his mother finally allowed the Prince to proceed to London. Edward IV had appointed as Protector of the Kingdom during the minority of his son his brother Richard of Gloucester, an exceedingly capable soldier who had so far been chiefly conspicuous for the unswerving loyalty and complete unscrupulousness with which he had served the late King, and who was generally suspected of having personally brought about the decease of Henry VI. Of her brother-in-law the Queen had always entertained a well-founded mistrust, and subsequent events proved only too abundantly that her shrewd suspicion that regicide was apt to become a habit was not without foundation.

The uncle came to meet his royal nephew on the

road to London, having arrested the two most prominent
of the Queen's relations, the Lords Rivers and Grey,
the previous night at dinner, and escorted his young
charge to his capital with every sign of affection and
respect. Arrived in London the King was first lodged
in the bishop's palace, but after a few days was transferred to the Tower. Meanwhile the Protector and his
cousin Buckingham packed the city with their armed
retainers and purged the Council of all undesirables in
a drastic and decisive manner. Having secured the
person of the little Duke of York and sent him to join
his brother in the Tower, Gloucester now embarked on
a campaign of ingenious but unconvincing propaganda.
Reports were circulated casting doubt on the legitimacy
of the young princes, and several noted preachers were
hired to deliver sermons explaining exactly why the late
King's marriage had been invalid, a difficult proposition
which even the most learned divines failed to argue
with much conviction. A few days later a deputation
arrived to beg Gloucester to take the Crown, to whose
pressing and unexpected request he at length unselfishly
acceded with an affecting and gratifying modesty. The
following month he was crowned and shortly afterwards
departed on a tour of his kingdom. During his absence
the two little princes were so unfortunate as to be
smothered in their beds, and their bodies were subsequently mislaid and were not rediscovered until the
reign of Charles II, when they were transferred to the
Abbey.

Edward V reigned the shortest time of any king of

England, and he was the youngest at the time of his death. Of his character not unnaturally singularly little is known, but he was well educated and is generally reported to have been amiable and unaffected. His fate, though tragic, can hardly be reckoned singular, for his great-grandfather, his grandfather, three uncles, his half-brother and his brother all ended their lives either at the hands of assassins or on the execution block.

RICHARD III
1483-1485

From a painting in the National
Portrait Gallery

RICHARD III 1483—1485

WHILE the career of Edward IV may perhaps be considered as providing yet another proof of the justice of the Psalmist's contention that the unrighteous are apt to flourish like a green bay-tree, that of his brother Richard assuredly demonstrates the fact the wicked do occasionally fall into a pit of their own making and that violent dealing does sometimes come down upon the pate of him who initiates it. A short time only elapsed after the murder of Edward V and his brother before Richard was faced with a dangerous insurrection led by his cousin and old ally Buckingham. Although their cause was good, the military skill of the rebels was much inferior to the King's and he experienced no difficulty in suppressing the outbreak and executing Buckingham. Having thus established peace throughout the kingdom he now tried to demonstrate by the excellence of his legislation that although his accession to the throne had been perhaps a trifle unconventional, his rule would be conspicuous for a natural clemency that he had hitherto been compelled by circumstances to suppress.

His subjects, alas, remained unconvinced and continued to regard their sovereign with the deepest mistrust : a sentiment which was considerably strengthened the following year by the death of his only son, a disaster which seemed to prove beyond a shadow of doubt that the hand of the Lord was against him. Eleven months later his wife died, and Richard, who well knew his precarious security was still further menaced by the absence of an heir, contemplated a second marriage. The bride whom he is reported to have selected as being the most suitable for his purpose was his own niece, Elizabeth, daughter of Edward IV and sister to the murdered princes. The mere suggestion of so incestuous and bloodstained alliance was, however, quite sufficient to alienate the sympathies of his remaining supporters and he was forced promptly to abandon the idea of this monstrous, but politically advantageous, union.

From now until the end of his reign, Richard was always uncomfortably aware that rebellion was likely to break out at any moment, and despite his tireless efficiency and numerous spies was never able to detect when and where the storm would burst ; that it would be Henry of Richmond who would ride the storm was only too obvious. The latter had gathered round him in France not only the last survivors of the Lancastrians but also Lord Dorset and others of the Dowager Queen's party whom Richard had been unable to liquidate, in addition to those of Buckingham's supporters who had been so fortunate as to escape. Well supplied with funds by the French King and in constant communication with many of those on whom Richard most relied, the conspirators could afford to wait their time. In August, 1485, they judged that the moment for action had come, and Henry landed at Milford Haven, where he was joined by many of his Welsh countrymen, while Richard collected his forces and marched west to meet his rival. The two armies confronted each other on the field of Bosworth, near Leicester, and in the ensuing battle Richard's military skill and personal bravery were insufficient to counterbalance the disloyalty of most of his own troops. Fighting desperately to the last he was eventually slain, and his crown, which he had been wearing over his helmet, rolled off into a holly bush whence it was subsequently retrieved and placed on the head of Henry of Richmond.

While Richard III was undoubtedly cruel, ruthless and tyrannical, it seems possible that his character was not quite so black as it was afterwards painted; he admittedly struck down without hesitation or remorse all who stood in his way, but his subsequent legislation was undoubtedly good, and one is not perhaps entirely justified in assuming that his anxiety for his subjects' welfare was altogether assumed. According to the standards of the time he was a clever and efficient Prince, and compared with his contemporaries, the Sforzas, the Borgias and the Medici a not outstandingly bloodthirsty one. Why was it, then, that his crimes aroused so long-lived a horror and proved to be so disastrous in their results whereas his brother Edward, who had eliminated his rivals, including the youthful son of Henry VI with as little compunction as Richard, should have died in his bed after a career which does not seem to have provoked in any marked degree the disapprobation of his fellows? The answer must surely lie in

Richard's personal appearance : the evidence of his portraits and his contemporaries both go to prove that his looks were undoubtedly against him. (He was not, however, probably hunchbacked as is generally supposed ; his affliction was no worse than a slightly withered arm, a disfigurement which has had a disastrous effect on the character of more than one monarch.) While Edward was famous for his handsome and pleasing appearance, the unfortunate Richard always looked the heartless villain he was, and presumably people were as apt to base their judgment on appearance in the fifteenth century as at any other time.

HENRY VII
1485-1509

*From a painting in the National
Portrait Gallery*

HENRY VII 1485—1509

HENRY VII is unique among our kings in that he appears never to have exhibited any ordinary human failings ; to have been not so much a crowned monarch as a cool and calculating intelligence seated on a throne. There is no indication that either love or hatred or any emotion ever influenced his conduct or that his actions were ever anything but the result of policy. Having from his earliest youth been constantly involved in situations which called for the highest degree of diplomacy and cunning, and having so frequently been forced to rely solely on his own unaided intelligence to preserve both his liberty and his life, he possessed at the time of his accession an understanding of the business of kingship such as few monarchs have managed to acquire after a long period on the throne ; alone of our sovereigns Charles II served a harder apprenticeship.

Henry's first action after his coronation was to marry Elizabeth, the daughter of Edward IV, thus strengthening his title to the Crown, and reconciling him to the remaining Yorkists. With those who had supported the late King and had fought at Bosworth he was remarkably forbearing ; not because he was by nature particularly clement, but rather because he was wise enough always to prefer a possible friend to a potential enemy and to realize that vindictiveness is seldom good policy. Although his right to the throne was not above dispute,

in one respect his position was a strong one ; for the
first time since the reign of Henry II the crown was free
from the menace of the great feudal barons, for the late
wars, while they had pressed less hardly than might
have been expected on the nation as a whole, had quite
broken the power of the few noble families they had
not exterminated. Thus the two rebellions with which
Henry was faced in the course of his reign drew their
support not from the nobility, but from the peasantry,
the Irish and from foreign powers. The first of these
occurred in 1488 and centred round the figure of a pretender. There were only two persons whose claims
could be considered possibly better than Henry's—the
Earl of Warwick, the son of that Duke of Clarence who
came to so sad and vinous an end in the reign of Edward
IV, and Edward de la Pole, a son of the elder sister of
Edward IV and Richard III. As the former had been
kept in the Tower for a considerable time, his appearance
was not generally familiar and the Duchess of Burgundy,
another sister of the late King, and her partisans had no
difficulty in imposing upon a credulous public a young
man named Lambert Simnel as the unfortunate Warwick. Supported by some Irish lords and a handful of
German mercenaries the luckless Simnel was landed in
Lancashire, where his expedition was easily defeated and
he fell into the hands of Henry, who, having paraded the
genuine Warwick through the streets in order to show
that there was no deception, relegated the misguided
impostor to the royal kitchens. Ten years later another
pretender appeared named Perkin Warbeck, who gave

out that he was the little Duke of York who had been
murdered in the Tower. This revolt was crushed as
easily as the last, but this time Henry did not repeat his
former clemency, and not only did he execute the
impostor Warbeck but also the luckless Warwick who
had played no part in either rebellion and whose only
fault was his royal birth.

The fact that the latter of these two revolts had
obtained a certain degree of support from the poorer
classes was an indication that Henry's rule, though strong
and just, was not altogether popular ; a result of the
diligence and efficiency with which he levied his numerous taxes. The King had fully realized that in the new
world that was rising from the ruins of the Middle Ages,
money was likely to have an importance that it had never
before possessed, and therefore pursued it with a tireless
and unflagging enthusiasm that was far from edifying.
With the able assistance of Cardinal Morton he succeeded in raising enormous sums from taxation, from
fines (his clemency was largely a result of his conviction
that a cash sum down was far more permanently gratifying than the blood of one's enemies) and from subsidies
from foreign monarchs. His love of peace, although
natural, was always fortified and rendered more reliable
by a monetary grant, and he succeeded in obtaining from
Charles VIII of France a far higher price for keeping the
peace than Edward IV had done from Louis XI. Apart
from its financial aspects his foreign policy was largely
determined by his eagerness to secure powerful and
judicious alliances, and he married his elder son Arthur

to the daughter of Ferdinand and Isabella of Spain, his daughter Margaret to James IV of Scotland, and on the death of his wife he himself engaged on an extensive but unsuccessful search for a second and suitably important bride.

He died in 1509 and left behind him a kingdom more settled and more prosperous than it had been for over a century, the last great achievement of Gothic architecture in this country and nearly two millions in hard cash. Few monarchs have achieved such substantial results with the exercise of so moderate a tyranny.

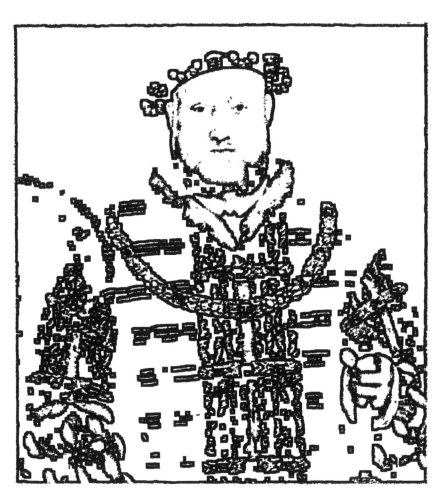

HENRY VIII
1509-1547

From a painting by Holbein in the
National Portrait Gallery

HENRY VIII 1509—1547

WHEN Henry VIII succeeded his father in 1509, the people of England were, for the first time, confronted with a typical product of the Renaissance. Both Richard III and Henry VII had been representative of certain aspects of the new order of things, but while they had possessed in full measure that quality of ruthless opportunism, that was so marked a feature of contemporary political practice, they were both lacking in the astonishing versatility which distinguished the great figures of the period, and which the new King displayed in a remarkable degree. Handsome, erudite, of enormous physical strength and gifted with a considerable talent for music and the arts, he promised at his accession to be the very paragon of the age.

While his elder brother was still alive, his father had entertained the remarkable idea of making Henry Archbishop of Canterbury, and with this end in view the young prince had been given a thorough grounding in the principles of theology. In later life he was to find in the knowledge he had thus early acquired, a weapon equally useful for the defence or the overthrow of the established principles of the Catholic religion. In 1501 his brother Arthur married Katherine of Aragon, the daughter of Ferdinand and Isabella of Spain ; seven years later Henry's first act after his accession was to lead his widowed sister-in-law a second time to the altar.

For the first twenty years of his reign, Henry was content to leave the administration in the hands of his great minister, Cardinal Wolsey. During this period foreign affairs assumed an importance they had not enjoyed for many years, largely owing to the young monarch's eagerness to play a prominent rôle on the European scene. This desire was gratified by the diplomatic skill of the Cardinal who obtained for his master a number of showy triumphs by his clever manipulation of the balance of power. This system of playing off the two strongest European powers against each other was Wolsey's greatest contribution to political theory and has ever since remained the foundation of England's foreign policy. Whether or not it provides a good reason for holding the Cardinal's name in reverence we are not yet, alas, in a position to say.

There was, however, one triumph that Wolsey with all his skill was unable to obtain for his master. Although Katherine had borne King Henry a daughter, their marriage had not yet been blessed by the arrival of a son. The difficult situation created by Henry's quite comprehensible feeling of annoyance at the continued frustration of this, his dearest wish, was further complicated in 1525 by the fact that the royal fancy had been caught by one of the Queen's ladies-in-waiting, Anne Boleyn, a niece of the Duke of Norfolk. At first the King showed no desire to place his connection with this lady on any permanent basis, but as the likelihood of his wife presenting him with an heir became ever more remote, the idea of a divorce recurred more frequently to his mind. It was an idea that had little or no appeal to the Cardinal, whose difficulties had, of late, been rapidly increasing. The vast sum left in the treasury by Henry VII had long ago been exhausted by his son, and in order to replace it Wolsey had been forced to adopt a variety of unpopular and largely illegal devices for raising funds. On his failure to obtain any satisfaction from the Pope in the matter of the divorce, the great minister was deprived of all his offices and was fortunate in anticipating an even worse fate by a fatal seizure (1530).

With the Cardinal dead, the King took matters into his own hands, and by virtue of his early theological training and with the assistance of favourable opinions from various Continental divines, he soon proved to his own satisfaction that his marriage with his brother's wife had been sinful, uncanonical and invalid. In 1533 he wedded Anne Boleyn, who presented him with a daughter in the short space of three months. The sex of this infant, however, completely annulled any sense of security that the new Queen may have fancied her wedding ceremony had guaranteed.

Having successfully defied the Pope in spiritual matters, Henry was soon tempted by the prospect of replenishing his empty treasury to challenge the rights of Rome in financial affairs. After transferring to his own pocket the annual tribute paid by the English Church to the Pope, he proceeded, ostensibly on purely moral grounds, to abolish the monasteries and confiscate their enormous estates. In order to invalidate any measures of a spiritual nature that the Pope might undertake against him, he had already taken the precaution of having himself proclaimed the Supreme Head of the Church in England (1536).

From now on a steady process of deterioration is observable in the character of the King, accompanied by, and perhaps not unconnected with, a slow but steady decline in his bodily health. In 1536 Queen Anne was executed on the charge of adultery, and several other prominent figures suffered a similar fate from time to time, for offences which, if less venial, were seldom more satisfactorily proved. A fortnight after the execution of Anne, Henry married Jane Seymour, who died a year later in giving birth to the longed-for son. In the same year a Catholic rising in the North was put down with considerable severity. In 1540, on the advice of Cromwell, Wolsey's successor, who was anxious to conclude an alliance with the Protestant powers on the Continent, Henry married by proxy Anne of Cleves, the daughter of an influential Protestant prince on the lower Rhine. His reactions on first seeing his bride were violent in the extreme and resulted in the prompt annulment of the marriage and the execution of the unlucky Cromwell. In the same year he married another niece of the Duke of Norfolk, Katherine Howard, whose moral character soon gave rise to suspicions no less grave than those which had brought her cousin to the block, and which soon involved her in a similar fate.

The physical discomfort and illness which troubled the King's remaining years were to some extent mitigated by the devotion of his sixth and last wife. Katherine Parr, a middle-aged widow of great strength of mind and such praiseworthy discretion that when Henry died in 1547 she survived to marry again a few years later.

The fact that Henry VIII was a tyrant is neither deniable nor particularly remarkable. What is, however, noteworthy, is that he was a highly successful one. Of all his gifts that which served him best was his astonishing ability to gage public opinion, a gift which prevented him from indulging in acts of despotism without having first ascertained that they would meet with a large measure of popular approval. If at his death he was more feared than loved, he could at least claim that, although he had on occasion excited the apprehension of his subjects, he had never forfeited their respect.

EDWARD VI
1547-1553

*From a painting in the National
Portrait Gallery*

EDWARD VI 1547—1553

IT is not unusual for claims to exceptional wisdom and virtue to be advanced on behalf of young princes who are cut off before their prime, but in Edward's case there seems to be some justification for such pious encomiums. Henry VIII's only son and youngest child was undoubtedly of an almost terrifying precocity. At the age of ten, when he succeeded to the throne, he was already conversant with seven languages, and is said to have found his chief delight in listening to the theological speculations of a variety of Protestant divines. However extraordinary his ideas of relaxation may seem, there is plenty of evidence to prove that he was an amiable and affectionate, though slightly priggish child.

The late King had, in his will, drawn up plans for a council of Regency to govern the kingdom during the minority of his son. In so doing it had been his object to prevent too much power from falling into the hands of the Earl of Somerset, the young King's uncle, of whose character he entertained a well-founded mistrust. Even Henry VIII, however, was unable to exercise much control from beyond the grave, and Somerset, by bribery and intimidation, soon succeeded in concentrating most of the power in his own hands.

The period of his regency was marked by two events of outstanding importance. In 1548 appeared the first

Book of Common Prayer, a volume that was as notable for the skill with which it reconciled all that was best in the doctrines of the Reformers with those ceremonies and rites of the Catholic Church which had been sanctified by tradition and long usage, as for the beauty of the style in which it was composed. The next year there occurred a rising in the Eastern counties which spread with lightning rapidity and at one time threatened to plunge the whole of East Anglia into a state of complete anarchy. Owing to the fact that the inhabitants of these counties were among the staunchest supporters of the new faith, the Protector Somerset failed at first to deal with the outbreak as ruthlessly or as effectively as he had dealt with a reactionary Catholic uprising in Devonshire in the previous year. Eventually, however, he was forced to take strong measures and the rebellion was crushed and its leaders hanged. The significance of this revolt lies in the fact that its causes were neither political nor religious, but economic ; the enclosures of common land and the rapacity of the new landlord class who had replaced the monastic orders had combined with a succession of bad harvests to cause widespread distress, particularly in Norfolk and Suffolk. Its aim was a complete social revolution of a scope and thoroughness that would to-day be considered Marxian ; its chief effect the sowing in the Eastern counties of the seed of that evangelical radicalism which was to bear fruit a century later and to flourish politically until quite recent times.

In addition to this civil warfare, the Protector had

also succeeded in involving the country in two foreign wars. In 1547 he invaded Scotland in order to force the Scottish court to fulfil their promise of sending their young Queen to England as a bride for Edward. Although the war was won, the objects for which it had been waged remained unattained, and the young Queen was sent to France to marry the Dauphin. This action promptly led Somerset to engage in war with France, in the course of which we lost Boulogne, the only conquest of Henry VIII.

Although the public undertakings of Somerset were disastrous enough, it was private animosity that brought about his downfall. In 1548 he had been compelled to imprison, and subsequently behead, his brother, who had been intriguing against him, and in 1550 John Dudley, Earl of Warwick, succeeded in persuading the King, largely by playing on his ultra-Protestant susceptibilities, that the time had come for his dismissal. In his place the King appointed John Dudley, Earl of Warwick, now Duke of Northumberland.

If Somerset had chastised the people with whips, Northumberland chastised them with scorpions. One of his first acts as Protector, and one, moreover, which aroused the greatest popular resentment, was to manipulate the currency in the most outrageous fashion and to his own great advantage. In 1552 he executed the unfortunate Somerset on a trumped-up charge of treason, and subsequently dealt as ruthlessly with all whom he fancied were in a position to threaten his authority. Somerset's greatest achievement, the first Prayer Book of Edward VI, he had already abolished in favour of a second version in which the extreme doctrines of the continental reformers found an honourable place (1550).

Early in 1553 it had become apparent to all that Edward VI was suffering from an incurable consumption and could not long survive. Having anticipated the speedy dissolution of the young king, Northumberland had already taken the precaution of marrying his son to the King's cousin, Lady Jane Grey, the granddaughter of Henry VIII's sister Mary. He now proceeded to persuade the dying boy to set aside the order of succession drawn up by Henry VIII, and to disinherit both Mary and Elizabeth in favour of his own daughter-in-law, and when in the summer of the same year the young King died, the Duke had perfected his plans for retaining his dictatorial position.

King Edward VI, although a shadowy and ineffectual figure, debarred by his youth and his ill-health from playing a large part in the affairs of his reign, did, however, in one respect, succeed in making his influence felt. Had he been less sincerely and less bigotedly attached to the Reformed Faith, the English Reformation would have been far less thorough-going than it was, and the two Protectors, more particularly the latter, would have lacked the requisite sanction for their arbitrary and despotic acts.

MARY I
1553-1558

*From a painting by Joannes Corvus
in the National Portrait Gallery*

MARY I 1553—1558

ON the death of Edward VI, Northumberland, having secretly proclaimed his daughter-in-law, Lady Jane Grey, Queen, made every effort to secure the person of the rightful sovereign, Mary, daughter of Henry VIII by his first wife, Katherine of Aragon. His failure to do so sealed his fate, for no sooner was the news of the King's death generally known than all sections of the community, both Catholic and Protestant alike, declared in favour of Mary, who was safely in the midst of a considerable body of armed supporters in Suffolk. Northumberland's army deserted and the Duke himself was forced to surrender and was executed in the Tower less than six weeks after the death of Edward VI.

When Mary succeeded to the throne she was thirty-nine years of age; although an upright and deeply pious woman, the neglect and contempt with which she had been treated in her youth had combined with her chronic ill-health to render her suspicious and morose. She was, alas, constitutionally incapable of retaining the loyalty and affection that her subjects had accorded her on her accession.

The new Queen's first action was to release all those Catholics who had been imprisoned during the two previous reigns; her second was to select for herself a Catholic consort and so deprive her sister Elizabeth, whose religious orthodoxy was gravely suspect, of the succession. Her choice fell on the Archduke Philip, the son of the Emperor Charles V and heir to the throne of Spain, a young prince chiefly remarkable for the zeal with which he professed the extremist Catholicism. The announcement of this marriage was the signal for risings all over the country, most of which the authorities experienced no difficulty in suppressing. One, however, led by Sir Thomas Wyatt in the staunchly Protestant county of Kent, was more successful and at one moment attained the dimensions of a considerable revolt, and it was only with some difficulty that it was eventually overcome and its leaders executed (1554). Its failure provided an admirable opportunity for disposing of the unfortunate Lady Jane Grey and her husband, who had been kept in imprisonment since the beginning of the reign. A further effort of the Catholic party was less successful; despite every ingenuity it was found impossible to implicate the Princess Elizabeth.

Having thus disposed of all open opposition, Mary proceeded with the plans for her wedding and was finally married to Philip in Winchester Cathedral in 1555. The marriage was disastrous from the first. Philip was a bigoted and ambitious prince, unacquainted with the English language and many years younger than his wife. Out of sympathy with English affairs and chiefly interested in continental politics, he soon neglected the unfortunate Queen, thereby increasing her already marked tendency towards hysteria and neuroticism. Left to herself Mary came to rely more and more on the one stay whose efficacy she had proved during her earlier years of ill-treatment—her ardent and uncompromising religious faith. This was doubly unfortunate, for not only was it a faith which the majority of her subjects did not share, but also one which led her to believe that to burn heretics was to acquire virtue. Despite the advice of many of her Catholic councillors and even of the bigoted Philip himself, she instituted the most rigorous and widespread persecution that this country has ever experienced. Bishops Latimer, Ridley and finally Cranmer were burnt at the stake, together with several other bishops and over three hundred of the laity. Many others were imprisoned and tortured and a still larger number forced to fly the country. The disgust aroused by these proceedings, combined with the unsatisfactory outcome of the war against France, into which Philip had persuaded Mary to enter, caused widespread discontent all over the country. Numerous conspiracies grew up around the person of the Princess Elizabeth, but, luckily for her, proved difficult to detect. Mary's last years passed in a sombre gloom illuminated only by the dull glow of flickering Protestants, and in 1558 she died, neglected by her husband, racked by disease, and detested by her people, alone with the comforts of that religion for which she had suffered so much.

Of all our monarchs Mary was perhaps the most consistently unhappy. In her youth she had been forcibly parted from her beloved mother, whose degradation she was forced to witness but forbidden to alleviate. As

a young woman she had been persecuted by her stepmother, neglected by her father and denied the consola-
tions of her religion by a bigoted brother. In middle
age she failed to gain the affections of a husband whom
she loved deeply, was prevented by her wretched health
from having the child for which she longed, and experienced the humiliation of losing Calais, the last remaining possession of the English Crown on the main-
land of Europe. She died with the bitter knowledge
that all she had done to re-establish the Catholic religion
had been of no avail, and that under her successor the
country was certain to revert to the heresy which she
had spent all her life opposing.

Mary's greatest mistake had been the Spanish marriage,
for after that event Roman Catholicism came to be
regarded as something worse than idolatrous—namely,
" un-English "—and henceforth its fate was sealed.

ELIZABETH
1558-1603

ELIZABETH 1558—1603

WHEN Elizabeth, at the age of twenty-five, succeeded to the throne of England, her political
ability had already been amply tested by the great
variety of vicissitudes and dangers from which she had
successfully emerged. During the reigns of her brother
and sister she had preserved both her life and her liberty
by her complete indifference to the questions raised by
theological controversy and her habit of going straight
to bed the moment that any crisis threatened. Her
attitude towards all religious matters remained unchanged
throughout her life, and to it may be attributed much of
the success with which she governed England during a
period when questions of dogma inflamed the passions
and destroyed the harmony of half the nations of Europe.

At her accession the gratitude and enthusiasm of her
subjects were almost her only assets, for the treasury
was empty, the Church detested, and the most powerful
of her potential allies estranged. Indeed the international position was one of considerable danger, as
Philip of Spain, on whose behalf England had gone
to war with France, was offended by Elizabeth's refusal
of marriage and might easily change from an unwilling
ally to an open foe. Moreover, the peace that had
hastily been concluded with France was likely at any
moment to come to an end as Elizabeth's heir, her cousin
Mary Queen of Scots, a great-granddaughter of Henry

VII, had married Francis II of France, and as a devout Catholic, regarded Elizabeth as illegitimate and usurping.

In dealing with these difficult matters the new Queen found, however, that she was not single-handed. In William Cecil and Walsingham she had two of the ablest and most devoted ministers that ever served an English sovereign. In 1560, on the death of Francis II, his widow returned to Scotland and his country was soon rent by civil and religious warfare. Thus Elizabeth and her ministers were in a position to turn their attention to such urgent matters as the reform of the currency and the stabilization of the Church.

Mary, on her return to Scotland, found herself faced with a situation of considerable difficulty, as during her absence a strong Protestant party had grown up who regarded their sovereign and her matrimonial vagaries with small approbation. The situation was not improved when, in 1567, her husband, Lord Darnley, was so unfortunate as to be blown up, and the widowed Mary promptly took as her third husband the unpopular Lord Bothwell, whose connection with the explosion was more than suspect. As a result of the openly expressed indignation of her subjects, Mary was forced to fly to England, where Elizabeth kept her in close confinement for the next twenty years.

In 1570 Pope Pius V formally excommunicated Elizabeth, and from that moment the Catholic party in England, who had hitherto enjoyed considerable freedom in matters of religion, were forced to choose between recantation and being regarded as potential traitors and assassins. Abroad the struggle between Catholic and Protestant was being waged with the utmost enthusiasm and ferocity, and Elizabeth was constantly being urged by the Protestant powers themselves, and by the same party at home, to intervene on their behalf. However, quite apart from the question of expense which she detested, Elizabeth entertained a wholesome unwillingness to afford any encouragement to subjects rebelling against their lawful sovereigns, however praiseworthy their motives.

At length, however, the time came when Elizabeth could no longer stand aloof. The assistance given by Spain to the various Catholic conspiracies that centred round the captive Queen of Scots, could not with safety any longer be ignored, and Elizabeth was forced to take extreme measures to secure her personal safety. In 1584 she sent an expedition commanded by her favourite Leicester to the Netherlands, and in 1587 she at length consented to the execution of the luckless Mary in Fotheringay Castle. The result of these actions was to force Philip of Spain, whose dominions in America had long been subject to the depredations of English privateers, to assemble an enormous fleet, christened the Great Armada, which set sail for England in 1588. Owing to the skill and bravery of the English seamen and to the unfavourable weather which it encountered in the Channel, and despite the fact that her natural parsimony led Elizabeth to keep her fleet in a far from well-equipped condition, this great armament was completely defeated, and although the war continued, Elizabeth's throne was never again in danger from foreign invasion.

Henceforward the Queen refrained from all but the most half-hearted intervention in foreign affairs, and the last fifteen years of her reign passed in a tranquillity that was undisturbed save for sporadic outbursts of violence and anarchy in Ireland. The circumstances of her death in 1603 were macabre in the extreme; for the last three days of her life she insisted, although mortally sick, on sitting fully dressed in the middle of the audience chamber refusing to speak, even to announce the name of her successor.

Vain, unscrupulous and mean, profoundly indifferent to all spiritual and æsthetic values (although intelligent and exceptionally well educated, the literary renaissance and the religious enthusiasm of her times left her equally unmoved), Elizabeth must yet be counted one of the very greatest of our sovereigns. The secret of her success lay in the fact that her conception of Kingship differed widely from that held by her predecessors, for she regarded herself as being, if not quite the servant of her people, at least their guardian. In her speech to her people on the eve of the Armada she said :

" Let tyrants fear : I have always so behaved myself, that, under God, I have placed my chiefest strength and safeguards in the loyal hearts and good will of my subjects."

The truth and wisdom of these words were amply proved by the popularity she enjoyed during her lifetime and the pride with which her memory is still recalled.

JAMES I
1603-1625

*From a painting by Paul Van Somer
in the National Portrait Gallery*

JAMES I 1603—1625

O N the death of Elizabeth the crown passed to King
James VI of Scotland, son of the unfortunate Queen
Mary and great-great-grandson of Henry VII. The
experience that this monarch had gained during the
years that he had spent trying to control the turbulent
nobles and fanatic presbyters in Scotland, had only
encouraged him in the formulation of numerous theories
of government without in any way increasing his ability
to deal with its practical problems. Affable, but devoid
of charm, erudite but singularly obtuse, weak when he
should have been firm, implacable when moderation
was indicated, James, at the age of thirty-five, was
remarkably unfitted for the high destiny to which he
had been called. As a foreigner he found himself
regarded with suspicion by his new subjects, and his
personal appearance did little to reassure them. Not
only was he clumsy and weak-kneed, but his tongue
was actually, as well as figuratively, an unruly member,
being far too large for his mouth, which gave him a
most unpleasant drooling appearance ; nor was the disgust which these physical peculiarities aroused in any
way dispelled by his thick northern speech and revolting
table-manners.

The new King's first action after his coronation was
to call a conference at Hampton Court (1604) to deal
with ecclesiastical affairs. During the latter part of

Elizabeth's reign the gulf separating the extreme Protestant party in the Church from those who stood by the Elizabethan settlement and were opposed to the abolition of those rites and ceremonies which had survived from Catholic times and which the continentally educated reformers regarded as idolatrous and superstitious, had been widening perceptibly. The conference which was summoned to bridge it gave little satisfaction to anyone save the King, who had always prided himself on his skill as a theological controversialist and was delighted with this opportunity for its exercise. The only result of this meeting was that the extreme Protestants seceded from the Church and formed numerous schismatic congregations of their own, while their opponents soon found themselves reduced to the position of civil servants, completely dependent on the King's will, not only in political but also in spiritual matters.

However the Protestants were not the only people who had occasion to regret James's excessive interest in religious questions, for on the chance detection of an elaborate plot on the part of several prominent Catholics to blow up the King together with Parliament assembled, the Papists were persecuted with deplorable, but comprehensible, ferocity (1605).

Despite the common danger which they had so providentially escaped, the King and his Commons were seldom on good terms, and as the reign wore on and James's conviction of the essential correctness of his favourite theory of the divine right of kings showed no signs of weakening, their relations became steadily worse. His fondness for Spain, the arbitrary nature of many of his acts, and his constant appeals for money gravely offended the political susceptibilities of his subjects, while their moral indignation was aroused by his numerous favourites, the extravagance and corruption of his court, and his notorious private life, which was sadly lacking in that orthodoxy for which his religious opinions were so conspicuous. On his death in 1625, having alienated public opinion, emptied the treasury, and considerably reduced his country's prestige abroad, he left his unfortunate successor naught but a crown the glory of which his actions had done much to diminish.

James's greatest mistake was his attempt to perpetuate the personal despotism of the Tudors as a permanent system of government, while failing to realize that the conditions which had justified and necessitated their arbitrary rule were no longer existing. Constitutionally incapable of inspiring loyalty or affection, and too conceited to appreciate their value, it was James VI's misfortune to succeed the most popular and best-loved monarch that had so far sat on the English throne.

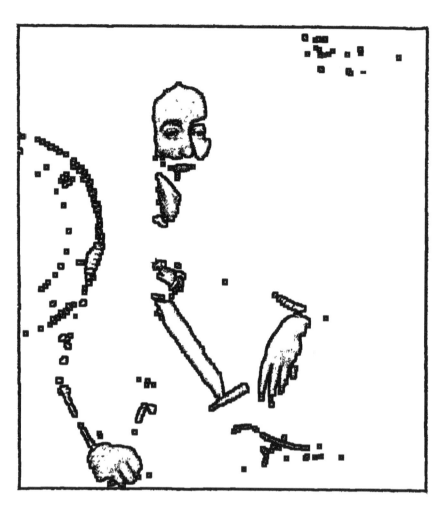

CHARLES I
1625-1649

*From a painting after Van Dyck
in the National Portrait Gallery*

CHARLES I 1625—1649

CHARLES I, the second and only surviving son of
James I, was in all respects save one, an almost
complete contrast to his father. Good-looking, courageous and strictly moral, his conviction of the divine
origin and extensive nature of his royal prerogative was
yet as firm and unshakable as the late King's, and in his
dealing with those who disagreed with him on this
point he did not hesitate to employ a craftiness and a
guile that were wholly foreign to his nature.

At his accession he was completely under the influence
of his father's favourite, George Villiers, Earl of Buckingham, a dashing opportunist, as unprincipled as he
was incompetent, who, in order to achieve the popularity that had so far eluded him, contrived to have
himself put in command of a remarkably unsuccessful
expedition against Spain (1623). The next year King
Charles, despite the fact that he had married a sister of
the French king and unmindful of the futile outcome
of Buckingham's previous military venture, entrusted
the wretched favourite with the command of an expedition to relieve the Huguenots of La Rochelle that proved
even more disastrous. These exploits had cost a great
deal of money and as James I had left nothing but debts,
the King found himself compelled to appeal to Parliament for funds. These, however, the faithful Commons
were only prepared to supply on certain conditions,

the chief of which was the dismissal of Buckingham. This the King refused even to consider and so, having dissolved Parliament, he proceeded to raise money by a variety of illegal and irksome devices. So bitterly were these measures resented that when Buckingham was assassinated at Portsmouth, where he was optimistically fitting out yet another military expedition, Charles discovered, on summoning a new Parliament, that much of the antagonism which the favourite had provoked was now directed at himself. Not until he had signed a Petition of Right presented to him by the Commons binding himself to refrain from various unconstitutional courses, could the King obtain the money of which he stood so badly in need. However, despite his royal signature, Charles almost at once began again to levy unauthorized taxes, and so great was the fury which this aroused that he was forced once more to dissolve Parliament (1629) and for the next eleven years he ruled the country without their assistance.

During this period Charles's two most stalwart supporters were Lord Strafford, who had abandoned his prominent position in opposition circles and gone over to the King, and Archbishop Laud, who saw in the rising power of Parliament a menace to the Established Church and an unwelcome support for the Calvinistic heresies of the extreme Protestants. While the King was busy devising more and more ingenious ways of raising money without the hateful necessity of summoning his Parliament, Strafford was subduing the Irish with a ruthlessness and savagery of which that unfortunate nation had hitherto thought none but themselves capable, and Laud was driving hundreds of the extreme Protestants out of the Church and into the arms of the nonconformists by the vigorous measures which he employed in a sincere but unwise desire to suppress all suspicion of unorthodoxy. It is significant that it was the distressing but tolerably legal proceedings of the sincere Laud rather than the dishonest practices of the shifty King or the high-handed brutalities of Strafford that brought about the final disaster. Not content with dragooning the English Church into obedience, the fanatical Archbishop tried to impose the Episcopal form of Church Government together with the English Prayer Book on the Presbyterian Church of Scotland (1636). The following year the whole of the Northern Kingdom rose in rebellion and Charles immediately set about collecting an army to force his Scottish subjects to obedience. So meagre and half-hearted was the resulting force that, having tried unsuccessfully to gain his ends by negotiation (1639) he was forced in 1640 to summon a Parliament to grant him the necessary supplies.

On their prompt refusal to do so, Charles as promptly dissolved them, and having raised what money he could by forced loans and other illegal devices, he departed at the head of an undisciplined and disaffected army to subdue the North.

By the end of the same year the King was back in London, his forces having been utterly routed in the North, where he was once more compelled to summon his indignant Commons. Their first action was to proceed against Laud and Strafford, both of whom the King made small effort to defend. The latter was beheaded in 1641 and the former imprisoned. This done Parliament then proceeded to make it impossible for Charles ever again to employ those methods of raising money on which he had relied in the past.

These salutary measures were not enough, however, to satisfy the reforming zeal of the Long Parliament, and they now proceeded to lay hands on the Church with the object of re-establishing it on Calvinistic lines. This move played straight into the King's hands for not only was a large section of the nation still loyal to the Church, but a formidable opposition was aroused among many of the members of Parliament themselves, so that when open hostilities broke out in 1642, Charles was able to count on the support of a very large number of his subjects.

During the first three years of the Great Civil War, neither side could claim to have gained any striking advantage; in the south and east the Parliamentary forces had been everywhere successful, but in the west and north the King's supporters were in the ascendant. It was not until the battle of Naseby in 1645 that Charles was finally doomed. After this crushing blow Charles fled to Scotland, preferring to entrust himself to the rugged honesty of the Covenanters rather than to the forces of the Parliament. Unfortunately for him so honest were his beloved Scots that, in return for a handsome financial consideration, they promptly handed him over to the men from whom he had fled. For a time Charles was kept in an honourable and far from stringent confinement, but as his efforts to profit by the dissensions that had broken out in the ranks of his enemies became increasingly obvious, and after he had made two unsuccessful attempts to escape, it was finally decided that the King must die. On January 30, 1649, after a farcical and disgusting trial, in the presence of a vast and strangely silent crowd, Charles I, dignified and courageous to the last, was beheaded outside his own palace of Whitehall.

Charles's good qualities were many, his faults were few, but circumstances had placed him in a position where his virtues availed him nothing and his defects were bound to involve him in disaster. In so far as he died in defence of his religious convictions he may justly be esteemed a martyr, but inasmuch as his execution was the result of his political actions he must be considered as being himself responsible for his tragic fate.

THE COMMONWEALTH

OLIVER CROMWELL 1653-1658
From the painting at Sidney Sussex College by Lely

RICHARD CROMWELL 1658-1659
From the painting in the National Portrait Gallery

THE COMMONWEALTH 1649–1660

OLIVER CROMWELL
RICHARD CROMWELL 1658–1659

ON the death of King Charles I in 1649 England found itself for the first time in its history without a monarch. Immediately after the King's execution Parliament had passed a measure declaring England to be a commonwealth and entrusting the powers of government to a reformed House of Commons and a Council of State. However, although Parliament might fancy that the control of the country's destinies was in its hands, all power had already passed to a military dictatorship, supported by force and inspired by evangelical fervour, of a sort to which recent events on the continent have fully accustomed the present generation, and the man who was actually in a position effectively to direct the course of events was Oliver Cromwell.

Early in 1645 Parliament had realized that owing to the comparative lack of success of the campaign in the previous summer, the time had come to effect far-reaching reforms in its military forces and that possibly a prominence in debate and a firm understanding of parliamentary principles were not always accompanied by a correspondingly high degree of military skill ; it was then decided that all those members of Parliament holding commands in the army should renounce them in

favour of professional soldiers who would be in a
position to give all their attention to military matters
undistracted by the cares of legislation. To this " Self-
denying Ordinance," as it was called, there was only
one exception ; the member for Huntingdon, Oliver
Cromwell, who had proved himself a cavalry general
of outstanding ability and who had organized the As-
sociated Counties, a military force drawn from East
Anglia which was to provide the model for the new
army, retained his commission. During the subsequent
course of the war, Cromwell had shown himself to be
a military genius of the highest order and his position
in the army, of which he was nominally only second in
command, soon became supreme. In 1647, while Parliament and the King were still haggling over terms, the
former suddenly woke to the realization that the New
Model Army which they had so cheerfully brought into
being was likely to prove a serious menace to their authority : for on several matters the army's point of view was
not that of Parliament. The Commons were staunchly
Presbyterian and eager for national conformity, whereas
the army was composed of men who held a startling
variety of religious views, among whom were many
who combined a thoroughgoing communism with doc-
trinal opinions of a luridly apocalyptic description.
Unfortunately for Parliament the revelation came too
late, and when they at length reached the decision to dis-
band it, the army already held the trump card—namely,
the person of the King—and flatly refused to be disbanded.
From that moment the direction of affairs passed out of

the hands of the Commons : a fact which at first they refused to recognize.

Most dictatorships are ushered in by some suitably dramatic demonstration, and this proved no exception. On the conclusion of the successful campaign of 1648, while Parliament was still carrying on futile negotiations with the King, the army decided that they must be made to realize who were now their masters. On the 6th of December a certain Colonel Pride marched down to the House at the head of his regiment and forthwith proceeded to arrest or expel all those members of whom the military disapproved. Pride's Purge, as it was called, may perhaps be regarded as the Reichstag Fire of the Commonwealth. It was immediately followed by the trial and death of the King.

The first task which confronted the new administration was the termination of the Civil War which still continued spasmodically in Ireland and Scotland. In the course of one campaign Cromwell reduced the former country more thoroughly than it had ever been reduced before, and having stamped out the last embers of revolt turned his attention to Scotland, where his arms soon proved equally successful. Having systematically overrun the country as far north as Perth, he returned to England in order to deal with the army of the Prince of Wales which had slipped across the border. At the battle of Worcester (1651) he completely defeated this last Royalist force and the Civil War was at length at an end.

The chief problem which engaged the attention of

Cromwell from now until his death ten years later was to produce some type of representative government which would carry out the wishes of the people without coming in conflict with his own. Like so many men of great force of character he found co-operation with others less gifted than himself difficult to achieve and, despite many and sincere efforts to govern through Parliament, was constantly forced to revert to a personal dictatorship which he would willingly have abandoned. During the next four years no less than five different varieties of government were given a trial, but only those which approximated to a military despotism with Cromwell as Lord Protector achieved any marked measure of success and none proved popular.

However, if the regime failed to arouse any marked enthusiasm at home, it soon made itself feared and respected abroad. In 1652, as a result of the passing of the Navigation Act, which dealt a deadly blow at the carrying trade of the Dutch, war broke out with that nation. Despite the fact that the English admiral, Blake, had gained his whole experience of warfare as a Colonel of Horse, he soon proved himself no mean naval commander and succeeded in sweeping the enemy from the seas. Three years later Cromwell declared war on Spain and relieved that decaying power of several of her most valuable colonies. So high a reputation did the English army now enjoy, that in 1657 Louis XIV was glad to avail himself of the assistance of a brigade of English regulars in his campaign in the Netherlands, and at the time of Cromwell's death, England occupied a more considerable position among the nations of Europe than she had for many years past.

When the great man died in 1658 the weakness inherent in all dictatorships at once became apparent : the lack of an equally gifted man to take the place of the deceased. The party which he had led was now promptly divided by personal jealousies and private feuds, and the hereditary expedient which was then resorted to which placed Richard Cromwell, a quiet retiring man, in his father's place soon proved useless. On the resignation of Richard it seemed possible that the Government would become the prey of a variety of ambitions and mutually antagonistic generals, and when the most powerful and disinterested of these, General Monk, took it upon himself to open negotiations with the exiled Charles there was general satisfaction. So ended England's one, and it is to be hoped only, experience of dictatorship.

CHARLES II
1660-1685

From a painting by Mrs. Beale
in the National Portrait Gallery

CHARLES II 1660—1685

ON his return from exile in 1660 Charles II was possessed of three great assets which enabled him to overcome the numerous difficulties with which he was then faced and many which subsequently arose during the twenty-five years he filled the throne—experience, intelligence and charm. His charm was natural, but his intelligence had been sharpened and his experience formed during the long period he had spent in the ante-rooms and on the backstairs of continental courts. His foreign upbringing and the constant intrigues in which he had been involved from his earliest years made him more than a match for our native politicians, and having waited so long for his kingdom he was in no danger of underestimating the value of patience.

So unpopular had the late government become that Charles's accession was everywhere greeted with the utmost enthusiasm, and so far from encountering any opposition, his first difficulty was to restrain the Royalist enthusiasm of his New Parliament. A singularly humane man himself, the King was far from sympathizing with the animosity which Parliament displayed towards the surviving figures of the Commonwealth. An Act of Oblivion and Indemnity had indeed been passed which absolved all those, save the actual regicides, who had taken part in the late disturbances, but in religious matters a far from tolerant outlook prevailed. By the Act of Uniformity (1662) all the clergy who refused to conform to the Anglican rites were deprived of their benefices, and in the following years numerous acts were passed depriving not only the ministers, but also the nonconformist laity, of innumerable civil and religious liberties. Charles realized that at the beginning of his reign, when the bitter memories of past indignities were still so fresh, it would be useless to attempt to modify this state of affairs, and it was not till 1672 that he issued his Declaration of Indulgence suspending the penal laws against Papists and Dissenters alike. But he was in advance of his time, for so great was the outcry both from the High Church and Low Church parties that he was forced to withdraw this admirable but wildly unpopular measure.

Charles's chief minister during the earlier part of his reign was Edward Hyde, Lord Clarendon, who had accompanied him during his wanderings in exile and whose daughter had married James, Duke of York, the King's younger brother and heir presumptive. This statesman's markedly pro-French sympathies, which his royal master shared to the full, involved the country in a war with Holland in 1665. Owing perhaps to the fact that the command of the fleet had been entrusted to two dashing cavalry generals, the war was attended by a quite conspicuous lack of success. Nor was this the only misfortune which befell the country at this time, for the same year the population of London was decimated by a most virulent plague. Over a hundred thousand people perished, and all who were able to do so fled to the country, with the exception of the King himself, who insisted on remaining in the stricken city. However, this disaster was counterbalanced in 1666 by the great fire which swept away most of mediæval London with commendable thoroughness and provided Sir Christopher Wren, the greatest of architects, with a splendid opportunity for supplying the country with a worthy and dignified capital ; an opportunity, alas, of which the parsimony of Parliament prevented him from making the fullest use.

The Dutch War was brought to an ignominious conclusion in 1667, and the disasters for which it had proved notable provided Parliament with the longed-for chance of getting rid of Clarendon. His place was filled by a clique of five noblemen, generally referred to as the Cabal. Charles viewed the change with equanimity as not only were they all his personal friends and well disposed towards a French alliance, but two of them were also avowed Papists and Charles was gradually tending more and more in the direction of Rome. By a secret treaty signed in 1670, the King bound himself, in return for a handsome subsidy, to assist his cousin Louis XIV in his ambitious designs on Holland, and the next year war broke out once more. In consequence of the unpopularity of this campaign and the outcry aroused by the Declaration of Indulgence, Charles was forced to dismiss his ministers and appoint in their place Lord Danby, a staunch Churchman. However, five years later, this nobleman's praiseworthy orthodoxy did not save him from impeachment when the part which he had played in the secret Treaty of Dover became generally known.

The remaining twelve years of Charles's reign were notable chiefly for the various Popish scares, usually quite unfounded, and for the first emergence of the two great political parties, the Whigs and the Tories. In 1685, with his customary dilatoriness, Charles died, leaving numerous children behind him, but none, alas, by his wife, Catherine of Braganza.

Although a notable wit and in his private life remarkably amorous, Charles was subject to frequent fits of melancholy and was far from being the merry monarch of tradition. Needless to say, his numerous amours, while sadly distressing many of his contemporaries and most historians, in no way detracted from his personal popularity which remained great throughout his reign. One of the cleverest of our kings, in face of considerable difficulties Charles II succeeded in obtaining for his country that quiet and ordered government which it so badly needed, and, having regard to the bloodstained records of the Tudors, the Bourbons, and the earlier Stuarts, much may be forgiven a man in his position and of his period of whom it was written,

Inclined to mercy and averse from blood.

JAMES II
1685-1688

*From a painting by Sir Godfrey Kneller
in the National Portrait Gallery*

JAMES II 1685—1688

JAMES II, who succeeded his brother in 1685, was a man of considerable ability but no judgment. The years of exile, which had proved so educative for his brother, he had employed in training to become a soldier and had served with distinction under the celebrated Turenne, and had seemed likely to do well in his chosen profession. After his brother's accession he had been given command of the Fleet, a post in which he displayed not only marked qualities of leadership but a decided talent for organization. An avowed Papist, he had been forced to relinquish his position at the time of the Popish Plot and to live once more in exile for several years.

Although a sincerely religious man and far more conscientious than his brother, he was entirely lacking in that humanitarianism for which Charles had been noted, and when, shortly after his accession, a rebellion broke out in the West of England, led by the Duke of Monmouth, a natural son of the late King and an ostentatiously staunch Protestant, he did not hesitate to suppress it with the most unnecessary ruthlessness. The ease with which he was able to overcome this ill-led and worse organized rising unfortunately gave him a quite erroneous impression of the strength of his position, and he thereupon proceeded to do all that lay in his power to further the Catholic cause in England. Like his father and his grandfather he entertained a highly exaggerated idea of the extent of the royal prerogative and employed it to override the decision of Parliament, who had passed a Test Act barring all Papists from public offices, and to appoint numerous prominent Catholics not only to commissions in the army and to University fellowships, but even to Church livings.

At first James's subjects seemed likely to acquiesce in these unconstitutional proceedings, for they well knew that the King was no longer a young man and that his heir, his elder daughter Mary by his first wife, Anne Hyde, was not only a firm Protestant but was also married to the champion of Protestantism on the continent, William of Orange ; but when his second wife, Mary of Modena, unexpectedly gave birth to a son, their attitude changed (1688). The inopportune arrival of this infant, which, although it took place in the presence of over sixty spectators, was commonly held to have been effected by a cunning piece of legerdemain with a warming-pan, coincided with a celebrated trial which was then exciting the public to a frenzy of indignation. The previous year James had ordered all the clergy to read from their pulpits a new declaration of indulgence towards the Papists. Archbishop Sancroft and seven other bishops not only refused to do so, but moreover sent the King a petition against the measure, whereupon they were promptly arrested and put upon their trial on a charge of publishing a seditious libel. Despite the fact that the court had been carefully packed they were all acquitted amid the most tumultuous enthusiasm.

For several years numbers of the more prominent Whigs had been intriguing with William of Orange, and they now decided that the moment had come to strike. Accordingly they sent him word to come over and dispossess his father-in-law and assume the crown. William, who had long been waiting for this opportunity, gathered together the largest army he could and set sail for England in the November of the same year. He landed at Torbay and, advancing towards London, was soon joined by many adherents. James got as far as Salisbury on his way to meet him, but despite the various concessions he had hastily made to Protestant opinion, was there forced by the numerous desertions from his forces to return to London, whence he fled by ship to France. The next year, provided with men and money by Louis XIV, James landed in Ireland where he was able to maintain himself for sixteen months, but was finally defeated by his rival at the Battle of the Boyne, 1690. The remaining years of his life were spent at the French court, where he divided his time between religious exercises and intrigues against his usurping son-in-law.

James II was not altogether a stupid man ; though far less intelligent than his brother he had a far greater capacity for work, and had his judgment been less warped by the bigoted nature of his religion, he was likely to have proved an efficient ruler. Naturally extremely gloomy (even his love-making was reported to have been very lugubrious), he became, in later life, exceedingly devout, and so great a reputation did he obtain for exemplary piety, that after his death in 1701 there was some talk of his canonization. But alas, with the traditional ill-luck of his family, he just failed to attain this posthumous compensation for the crown he had forfeited on earth.

MARY II
1688-1694

From a painting by William Wissing
in the National Portrait Gallery

MARY STUART, who was born in 1662, was the daughter of James II by his first wife, Anne Hyde, daughter of Lord Clarendon. Together with her younger sister Anne, she was brought up as a Protestant and throughout her life displayed no leanings towards the faith of her father. She developed into a devout but excessively sentimental young woman, vivacious and pleasing in appearance but inclined to plumpness. During the period when her uncle, Charles II, and his ministers were on such close terms with Louis XIV, there was much talk of marrying her either to the Dauphin or the King of Spain, but finally the frequently expressed antipathy of his subjects for the Papists and all their works convinced Charles that William of Orange would prove a far more suitable husband for his niece.

The first years of Mary's married life were far from happy, for her husband was a silent and ambitious man to whom any display of emotion was neither natural in himself nor congenial in others. Entirely wrapped up in his ambitious schemes for thwarting the King of France, he was frequently away from home for long periods, and his wife was forced to accustom herself to a certain degree of neglect. He was not, however, incapable of gratitude, and after Mary had relinquished her rights to the English throne in his favour, there was a considerable improvement in their relations. All her life she was devoted to her husband and her greatest sorrow was caused by her inability to provide him with children. Of her father she disapproved on religious grounds and although, even after his deposition, James continued to correspond with his younger daughter, he could never bring himself to forgive Mary.

On her return to England as Queen, Mary found herself forced to undertake numerous public duties for which she had little inclination, and to maintain a state to which she had long been unaccustomed and now found irksome. During the King's frequent absences abroad she acted as regent, and though she had little aptitude for public business she conscientiously transacted it to the best of her ability. Not the least of her difficulties arose from the conduct of her sister Anne, who was constantly indulging in spiteful and petty intrigues with her friends the Churchills. As she grew older her health, which had never been robust, became steadily worse, and she turned more and more towards the comforts of religion. Although at the time of her accession she had aroused considerable criticism by what was considered the highly inappropriate levity of her behaviour on entering her unfortunate father's palace, but which was in fact merely her normal vivacity asserting itself on what she quite understandably considered to be a joyful occasion, she was subsequently well liked by the majority of her subjects. Her popularity was an invaluable asset to her husband, who was never able to command a more than doubtful loyalty and singularly little affection. She died in Kensington Palace of the smallpox in 1694.

A worthy but undistinguished figure, overshadowed by her celebrated husband, she always did what she was told, and moreover did it very well. If she has few claims to greatness, she was at least deserving of high praise for the skill and discretion with which she played her secondary but important rôle. On the affections of Londoners she has a lasting claim, for it was she who made the Serpentine, and it remains her only memorial.

WILLIAM III
1688-1702

WILLIAM OF NASSAU, Prince of Orange and Stadtholder of the Netherlands, was the posthumous son of William II of Orange and Charles I's daughter Mary. Although the family of Nassau had held the position of Stadtholder for over a century it was not then an hereditary office, and William III did not obtain it until he was twenty-two and in command of his country's forces at the time of the third Dutch War. Peace was made with England in 1674 but not with France, and henceforth his personal rivalry with Louis XIV was the dominating note of William's life. In order to secure England's alliance in his struggles, he came to London in 1677 to propose for the hand of James's daughter the Princess Mary. His suit was very acceptable to English public opinion, though less so to the Princess's father and uncle, and his efforts were crowned with success.

Firmly allied to the two principal Protestant powers in Europe (his wife was the heir-apparent to the English throne and he himself was the nephew of Frederick William the Great Elector), William could afford to overlook the unfavourable clauses of the Treaty of Nimeguen, by which peace had been made in 1678, and to concentrate on preparing for a renewal of the struggle in the near future. At first his relations with his father-in-law were exemplary, and on the occasion of Monmouth's rebellion he not only refused all aid to the rebels but actually sent James warning of their intentions. It is possible that he was not quite so disinterested as he maintained, for Monmouth had proclaimed himself a legitimate son of Charles II, and had his rebellion been successful, Mary would automatically have been deprived of the succession. Moreover, with Monmouth out of the way, William could be certain of there being no rival in the rôle of deliverer in the event of deliverance being necessary.

As James's conduct became increasingly provocative the necessity became more and more apparent, and William laid his plans accordingly. In 1688 the moment arrived, and, exclaiming "Now or never," the Prince of Orange set out for England with a remarkable army of 40,000 men, including Dutch, Swedes, Swiss, Negroes, and 200 Laplanders. At first it seemed likely that William would be disappointed in the help he had counted on obtaining from the English themselves, but as he advanced farther east the population overcame their understandable reluctance to fight for their ancient liberties shoulder to shoulder with Blackamoors and Laps, and adherents flocked to his banner in ever-increasing numbers.

Once James had fled the question immediately arose as to what William's future position should be; the prospect of being merely a prince consort he at once rejected, and the idea that he and his wife should act as regents for the departed King was not one which he could seriously consider. Finally, it was decided that

William and Mary should both be crowned and that Mary should delegate her executive powers to her husband for life. At the same time Parliament, by the Declaration of Right, reaffirmed all those liberties and rights which James II had overridden, and by an Act of Settlement confirmed the succession in the Protestant line. Having defeated the forces of his father-in-law in Ireland in 1690, William could at length consider his new position secure.

William's subsequent relations with Parliament soon degenerated into an unending wrangle over the question of this country's participation in his constant efforts to crush the power of France, and it was not until Louis XIV had foolishly provoked England's justifiable resentment by his recognition of James II's son as the lawful king on the death of his father, that William could at last depend upon the whole-hearted support of his new subjects in his foreign policy. By then, alas, it was too late, for the unfortunate King had no sooner completed his arrangements for a final campaign, which ultimately resulted in the complete victory of the allies, than he fell from his horse near Hampton Court and died a few weeks later.

The Whigs had invited William to this country purely to satisfy their own interests, and he had accepted in order to serve his own. In these circumstances it is surprising that a workable compromise was ever arrived at. Gloomy, foreign and suspicious, compelled, by the asthma from which he suffered, to avoid the capital, it is hardly astonishing that the King was never popular and that his great qualities were generally underestimated. On the other hand his principal ministers, such men as Danby and Churchill, with their long record of consistent treachery, could hardly complain if their sovereign preferred to rely largely on his own judgment and his Dutch advisers.

ANNE
1702-1714

*From a painting by John Closterman
in the National Portrait Gallery*

ANNE 1702—1714

QUEEN ANNE, who succeeded William III in 1702, despite the fact that her reign coincided with one of the most glorious periods in our history was herself a woman of even fewer talents than her sister Mary.

In 1683 she had married Prince George of Denmark, a character so defiantly colourless that few people seem ever to have been aware of his existence. Charles II remarked on one occasion that he had tried him drunk and tried him sober, but there was nothing in him either way. As a husband, however, he proved himself kind, affectionate and remarkably persevering ; in the course of their married life Anne was brought to bed of no less than ten or eleven miscarriages and four children, none of whom survived for more than a few years.

At her accession and for the first eight years of her reign Anne was completely under the influence of her childhood's friend Sarah Churchill, the wife of the celebrated general, who had little difficulty in persuading her mistress to continue the war against France for which William III had so carefully prepared. Personal inclination led the Queen to give the command of her armies to her favourite's husband, whom she soon made Duke of Marlborough, and never was an act of royal favouritism so abundantly justified by the results. In a generation which numbered such celebrated warriors as Prince

Eugene and Charles XII of Sweden, Marlborough was universally admitted, both by his contemporaries and by posterity, to have been pre-eminent in military genius. Under his command the allies were everywhere successful, and the victories of Blenheim, Ramillies, Oudenarde and Malplaquet not only lent lustre to a reign that otherwise would have been sadly undistinguished, but also widely extended the foreign possessions of the crown and gave England the stronghold of Gibraltar and control of the western Mediterranean.

Glorious as were these successes, they by no means commanded universal approval. The prestige and influence which they gave to the Marlboroughs were bitterly resented by the Tories, who had long been intriguing against the favourite and her husband. In Harley and Bolingbroke the opposition possessed two leaders of outstanding brilliance and complete unscrupulousness who did not hesitate to employ the Duke's well-known weakness over money matters as a weapon with which to discredit him. In 1711 their intrigues were at length successful, and the great general was deprived of his command and his wife dismissed from all her court appointments.

From now until the end of the reign the question which dominated all others was that of the succession. The Protestant heirs, the aged Electress of Hanover and her son, were known to favour the Whigs, which led many of the Tories to intrigue with James II's son, the old Pretender. Anne herself was thought to have a weakness for her half-brother, and could never bring herself to allow the Electoral Prince to pay her a visit. On James's repeated refusals to contemplate changing his religion, many of the moderate Tories abandoned his cause, but not so Bolingbroke, who knew that his own political life depended on the exclusion of the Hanoverians. Unfortunately for him the Queen died before he had completed his plans, and the peaceful accession of the Protestant heir was easily secured.

Despite her personal insignificance Anne's reign was one of the greatest periods of our history ; the military successes for which it was distinguished were paralleled both in literature and the arts. The Queen herself, although the contemporary style of domestic architecture is popularly called by her name, was in no way responsible for this second renaissance. Dull, greedy and inclined to be sly, Anne is neither a memorable nor a particularly attractive figure. She was, however, kind and charitable, especially towards the over-prolific, for whose misfortunes she naturally felt a personal sympathy, not perhaps unmixed with envy.

Anne was the last English sovereign ever to preside at a Cabinet meeting, and the last to touch for the King's Evil.

GEORGE I
1714-1727

GEORGE I 1714—1727

FEW men have been more heavily indebted to their mothers than George Louis of Brunswick-Luneburg, Elector of Hanover and King of England, for not only did he owe to her what little knowledge of statecraft he had been able to acquire, together with a certain inherited shrewdness, but also his title to the English throne. The Electress Sophia of Hanover, daughter of the unfortunate Princess Elizabeth, the "Winter" Queen of Bohemia, and granddaughter of James I, found herself on the death of Queen Anne's last surviving child, next in the line of succession by virtue of the Act of Settlement. Much to her disappointment, her cousin Anne, who had never enjoyed her robust health and whom she had always despised, outlived her by a few weeks, and so, in 1714, her son was called upon to wear the Crown which she had coveted for so long.

George Louis was then fifty-four years of age, and there had so far been nothing in his career to distinguish him in any way from a score of contemporary German princelings. He shared with them a passion for the military life and had served with some distinction in the Turkish wars under Prince Eugene and in the Low Countries with William of Orange. He was unprepossessing in appearance, and there was little in his character to belie his looks. In 1682 his parents had married him to his cousin Sophia Dorothea, Princess of Zelle ; a marriage that proved disastrous to both parties. He treated his young wife with considerable brutality for several years and finally, when she had borne him two children, banished her to the Castle of Ahlden, where she remained in the strictest confinement until her death thirty-four years later.

George's arrival in England, despite the general satisfaction at the failure of the Jacobite intrigues of the extreme Tories, was greeted with little or no enthusiasm, and throughout his reign he did nothing to achieve the popularity that had been denied him at his accession. His subjects were never of the opinion that to know him was to love him, and the bad impression created by the long train of favourites he brought with him from Germany at the beginning of his reign was only strengthened as his partiality for Hanover and the rapacity of his character became more and more apparent. In these circumstances it says much for his natural shrewdness that he contrived to remain comparatively firmly on a throne to which a large proportion of his subjects considered he had no legal right.

The new King had seen at once that he had only been chosen by the Whigs as the lesser of two evils, and that any line of action initiated by him would be certain to offend at least half the country. He was therefore only too happy to leave the conduct of affairs in the hands of his ministers and to transfer to their shoulders the responsibility for the success or failure of the policy of the Crown. His unwillingness to take part in any political discussions was not unnaturally increased by his total inability to understand the language in which they were carried on. Such were the humble origins of the theory of ministerial responsibility, the very corner-stone of our Constitution.

However, if George I showed small desire to exercise his prerogative in great matters he soon realized its usefulness in small ones, and so contrived to make his sojourn among us not unprofitable financially. Indeed the shamelessness with which he and his favourites lined their pockets with the proceeds of the sale of offices, titles and even bishoprics did much to increase the contempt in which he was popularly held. Moreover, it formed a disastrous precedent for corruption, the effects of which were destined to be felt throughout the century.

His last years were, if not saddened, at least rendered uncomfortable by the bitter animosity with which he quarrelled with his son, thus setting another unfortunate example that was only too faithfully followed by his descendants.

His end was sudden and appropriate. He died on the night of June 12th, 1727, in his coach on the road to Osnabrück from a paralytic seizure brought on by the exceptionally rough crossing that he had insisted on making in his frantic eagerness to get to his beloved Hanover.

After his death he is said to have revisited his mistress the Duchess of Kendal at her apartments at Hampton Court in the form of a black crow.

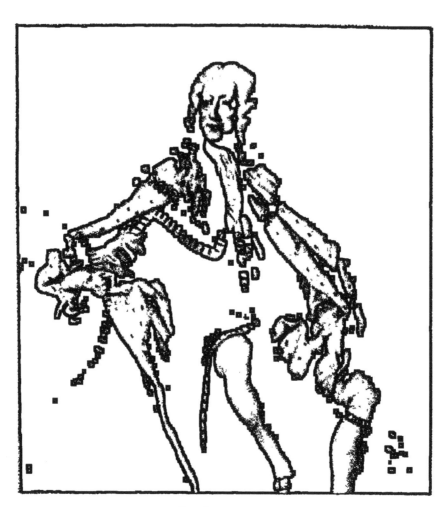

GEORGE II
1727-1760

*From a painting by Thomas Hudson
in the National Portrait Gallery*

GEORGE II 1727—1760

WHEN George II succeeded to the throne in 1727 he had for some years previously enjoyed a considerable measure of popularity. This was due not, it must be confessed, to any particular virtues of his own but rather to the fact that he had for some time been in open opposition to his father, whose death had been regarded by all his subjects as a providential relief too long delayed. Despite the fact that the new King had recently been on the worst possible terms with his parent, the characters of father and son had none the less many points of resemblance. Both were courageous, avaricious and utterly selfish, but whereas George I had been cold and calculating, George II was hot-tempered and incapable of dissimulation ; although regarded from a strictly moral standpoint their private lives were equally reprehensible, George II derived a certain advantage from the fact that his mistresses were usually English and therefore his lapses from virtue aroused less indignation among his patriotic subjects. Moreover, he was exceptionally fortunate in his wife, Caroline of Anspach, one of the most intelligent and charming Queens who ever sat beside her husband on the English throne. This tolerant and witty woman always turned a blind eye to her husband's numerous infidelities and, what was far harder, forced herself to listen sympathetically to his rambling and tedious confidences at all hours of the day and night ; as a result she never lost his love and was always consulted by him in all matters of importance.

However, although George II in the rôle of husband was a tolerable success, as a father he proved himself as lamentable a failure as the late King. His detested parent was scarcely cold in his grave when George startled his courtiers with the gratifying piece of information that he regarded his own eldest son, Frederick, as " the greatest beast, the greatest liar and the greatest fool in the world."

Thus the political situation of the last reign was now repeated, for George, on the advice of his wife, continued in office his father's great minister Sir Robert Walpole, while the opposition once more centred round the Prince of Wales.

For the next ten years Walpole's friendship with the Queen was of inestimable benefit to him, for his relations with the King never achieved any marked degree of cordiality : George, incurably pugnacious, was always longing for a satisfying war, whereas the whole object of Walpole's policy was the maintenance of peace. At length in 1739, two years after the death of Caroline, Walpole was forced by public opinion, much against his will, to embark on a colonial war with Spain, the results of which were disastrous and brought about his resignation two years later. The new ministers, Carteret and Pelham, were far more willing to gratify their master's desire for military fame, and in 1742, on the outbreak of the war of the Austrian Succession, they readily acquiesced in England's participation on the side of the unfortunate Maria Theresa. This gave George the opportunity for which he had been longing, not only to display his martial prowess but also to score off Frederick the Great, the son of his brother-in-law Frederick William, with whom he had been quarrelling for years, and he now departed for the continent at the head of his army.

In the campaign of 1743 George found himself confronted by a French force twice the size of his own at the village of Dettingen in South Germany. Placing himself at the head of his troops the gallant King marched straight at the enemy whom he succeeded in completely defeating and driving into the waters of the Main. This triumph, the last occasion on which a king of England led his troops into battle in person, enormously increased George's popularity. Two years later he displayed a similar though less dramatic courage at the time of the Forty-five. In that year Prince Charles Edward, the grandson of James II, landed in Scotland at the head of the last Jacobite expedition, and receiving a considerable measure of support in the Highlands he marched as far south as Derby. The King and most of his troops were abroad at the time, but when the news reached him George hurried back to England, where his coolness and determination did much to arrest the general panic. Shortly afterwards the Jacobites were completely defeated at the battle of Culloden, and the English throne was never again menaced by a Pretender. Eleven years later war with France broke out once more, but George was now an old man and left the fighting to "black men on the coast of Coromandel" and "red men by the Great Lakes of North America."

He died in 1760 before this colonial warfare had been brought to its triumphant conclusion.

There was about George II a certain dash and absence of guile which saved him from cutting so unattractive a figure as his father. Although coarse-grained and completely unimaginative, his letters to his wife, from whose death in 1737 he never recovered, reveal a streak of ingenuous and sincere affection which renders their writer an almost attractive and rather pathetic figure. With all his faults the man who could inspire so genuine and so constant a devotion in such a woman as Queen Caroline cannot have been wholly unworthy of our admiration.

GEORGE III
1760-1820

*From a painting by Allan Ramsay
in the National Portrait Gallery*

GEORGE III 1760—1820

THE young man who now succeeded his grand-father, despite the fact that he had not had a single ancestor born in England for nine generations, was to prove one of the most typically English Monarchs that ever wore the crown. Speaking English with a native accent, a feat which only a small minority of our sove-reigns since Elizabeth had accomplished, at his accession George III assured his gratified subjects that he gloried in the name of Briton : his subsequent career fully justi-fied his patriotic claim although it did not lack occasions which were not perhaps so conspicuous for glory.

Conscientious, ambitious and far more intelligent than many of his critics, both contemporary and subsequent, were willing to credit, the young King was determined personally to direct his country's government and to abandon the subsidiary position to which their ignor-ance of, and lack of interest in, English affairs had rele-gated the last two monarchs. The methods by which he was able successfully to maintain his personal rule for nearly twenty years are proof both of his skill as a judge of character and his ability to profit by the mistakes of his predecessors. He made no attempt to suspend the constitution and was content to rule through his parliament ; but it was always a parliament that he had taken the precaution of bribing. Thus he was able to mask his autocracy behind a constitutional façade, an advantage of which the Stuarts had never been in a position to avail themselves. He was not at first completely successful, and it took several years and much money before he was able finally to consolidate his power, but in 1770, profiting by the dissensions which divided the Whigs, George was at last able to appoint as Prime Minister his own protégé, Lord North, a pliant and unenterprising man.

The next ten years were spent in futile and untiring efforts to maintain the disastrous North in office in face of the relentless opposition which his catastrophic mishandling of the nation's affairs so justly aroused. In 1775 war broke out in America. The British Government had held the reasonable view that the colonists, as they derived considerable benefits from British rule, should bear some of the expense which it entailed, and had accordingly imposed taxation : the colonists, quite understandably, maintained that they would not submit to taxation without representation. As it was manifestly impossible for the colonists to send members to Westminster, the issue was actually whether or not the colonies should be taxed. Under the direction of the King and his minister the resulting war was as grossly mismanaged as the negotiations which might have prevented it, and after two years England found herself faced not with a mere handful of revolting colonials, but with a powerful and dangerous combination of France, Spain and an independent America. The fact that in 1783 when peace was made our territorial losses, apart from the American colonies, were comparatively slight was entirely due to good luck and the bravery and skill of individual naval and military commanders and reflected no credit on either the sovereign or his administration. After this disaster it was impossible for the King to continue personally to direct his country's destinies through the medium of carefully selected ministers, and in 1784 the Premiership passed to William Pitt, the brilliant and industrious son of the great Lord Chatham, who by his financial and parliamentary skill succeeded in restoring his country's fortunes in an unexpectedly short time.

Although at first George III regarded Pitt as only one degree less objectionable than the various Whig leaders, he soon became reconciled to his great minister, and suspicion gave way to mutual esteem. The harmony of their relations was, alas, considerably disturbed in 1788, for in that year the King went mad and although he soon recovered, the possibility of a recurrence of the malady created numerous difficulties for Pitt : for it soon became obvious that if the King was forced to give his consent to legislation to which he was violently opposed that possibility would become a certainty. Thus Pitt was forced to choose between abandoning such measures as Catholic Emancipation or imposing upon the country the irresponsible and supposedly Whig Prince of Wales as Regent. Naturally, being under no illusions as to the character of the Prince, Pitt chose the former.

The Prince of Wales, who had been submitted by his parents to an educational scheme of unenlightened and monotonous strictness, did much by his behaviour to

render unhappy the few years of comparative sanity
that remained to his unfortunate father, whom the
appalling events of the French Revolution and the subsequent wars had shaken and depressed. In 1810 the
old gentleman was observed by his attendants to make
a habit of saluting one of the oaks in Windsor Park
under the impression that it was the King of Prussia,
in itself a pardonable error, but when considered in
conjunction with various other distressing delusions, of
which the most remarkable was that all marriages had
been summarily dissolved, could only lead to the conclusion that the royal reason was once more tottering.
The last years of George III were gloomy in the extreme ;
blind and mad and, alas, frequently aware of his pitiable
condition, his sole relaxation was music, and for ten long
years the silence of Windsor was only broken by the
faint strains of Handel echoing from the royal organ,
until at last in 1820 the aged monarch found a final
release from his sufferings.

Kindly, religious and devoted to his wife, the simplicity and unblemished virtue of "Farmer George's"
private life was in marked contrast to that of his immediate predecessors, and while it caused him to be
regarded as a comic figure by the nobility it firmly
endeared him to the rising middle classes.

Politically he suffered from the firm conviction that
he was fully capable of superintending all the innumerable details of administration himself, a delusion which
cost him his reason and his colonies. Genuinely anxious
for his country's welfare he was always firmly of the

opinion that he alone was in a position to judge what constituted it, and his efforts to prove the truth of this supposition to his obstinately incredulous subjects lost him much of the popularity that had been his at his accession, and only when he was finally and irremediably mad was he once more firmly reinstated in the affections of his people.

GEORGE IV
1820-1830

*From a painting by Sir Thomas Lawrence,
P R.A., in the National Portrait Gallery*

GEORGE IV 1820—1830

THE character of George IV has probably evoked less admiration than that of any of our monarchs save John ; moreover, he has even been denied the compensating glamour that attaches in retrospect to those who were really wicked in a spectacular way, for the age in which he lived and the constitution by which he was bound prevented him, had he been so minded, from indulging in those vices which achieve the dignity of horror and only encouraged him in persevering in those which are apt to prove expensive. His private life and his public extravagance were the two things for which he was chiefly condemned, and the fact that thrift and fidelity to marriage vows were the two virtues which the succeeding generation insisted on to the exclusion of all others, rendered it inevitable that his memory should henceforth be held in the greatest contempt. He was held up as a bad father, a bad husband and a bad son, and it would be impossible to maintain that he achieved any marked success in any of these rôles. However, it is equally true that he had an unsympathetic father, an infuriating wife and a stubborn child ; in addition he had a debauched and good-for-nothing uncle who must share with George III the credit for much of his disgraceful behaviour as a young man. Thwarted and antagonized by the strict regime in which his father foolishly sought to confine him, George was only too happy in the company of the Duke of Cumberland and his discredited Duchess, than whom none could have exposed the young prince to a greater variety of deplorable influences.

His public career started under far more favourable auspices, for it was Fox himself who encouraged George to give his support to the Whigs, but despite this splendid beginning the outcome was sadly disappointing, especially for the Whigs, for once George attained to power he showed himself as reactionary as his father, and his old friends were left grumbling in the wilderness. For this great betrayal the Whigs themselves were largely to blame, for it is always bad policy to encourage the heir to the throne to engage in politics, and sheer lunacy when he is so conspicuously lacking in political ability as was George. However, they could draw comfort from the fact that as a supporter he would undoubtedly have proved a constant burden and deprived them of one of their most useful sticks with which to beat the Tories; for nearly thirty years defending the eccentricities and coping with the debts of George III's high-spirited offspring were among the most difficult and constantly recurring of the Government's tasks. Even when they were exceptionally able and intelligent, the Tory party could well have dispensed with the support of these worthies, and to Ernest, Duke of Cumberland, was due much of the antagonism which finally drove the party from office.

The factor which contributed more largely to George's unpopularity during his lifetime than any other was his disastrous marriage. It is possible, as her supporters maintain, that Caroline of Brunswick would have made a good wife had she been accorded the right treatment, but it is highly improbable that she would ever have found a husband with sufficient tact, forbearance and patience to administer it. Stupid, badly dressed and defiantly frolicsome, a worse wife for George IV could hardly have been found and, moreover, he was in the unusual but difficult position of having married her for his father's money; for George III had made the payment of his son's debts conditional on his marrying. Though his subsequent treatment of Caroline was unjustifiably brutal it was therefore hardly unexpected. Needless to say the sympathies of the people were hers from the very beginning, for she had just that sort of comico-pathetic appeal that goes straight to the heart of the British public. George's unsuccessful and ill-considered action in pressing for a divorce did much to render him detestable to his subjects as Regent, while his exclusion of his wife from the ceremony of his coronation was an unfortunate and much publicized beginning to his career as king.

Politically King George IV was an almost negligible element, for save for an unexpected enthusiasm for the Protestant religion which led him resolutely to oppose any measure for Catholic Emancipation, he had no very marked political convictions. Staunchly patriotic, he took a proper pride in the great military and naval successes his country achieved during his lifetime, and had his domestic life been more savoury and his lack of popularity less apparent he would have made a splendid and dignified figure-head for England during this glorious period.

In the arts, particularly architecture, he displayed a genuine though opulent taste, and he deserves our gratitude for his reconstruction of Windsor Castle, the encouragement he gave to the town-planning schemes of the architect Nash and for the discovery of Brighton. In addition, he possessed all the social graces and was universally admitted to be a charming companion ; his conversation was witty and entertaining and his imitations justly renowned. In his personal relationships he exhibited a truly royal inconstancy, and though affable and full of charm his insincerity was never called in question. In 1830, fortified by cherry brandy and the company of Lady Conyngham, he passed away amid the expensive rusticity of his cottage at Windsor, regretted by none save those under sentence of death in whom he had been accustomed to take a compassionate and frequently successful interest. Had he been born a contemporary of Louis XIV and inherited some continental crown it seems probable that he might have proved a memorable though eccentric ruler, although it is highly unlikely that any country save England could have afforded so fantastically extravagant a sovereign.

WILLIAM IV
1830-1837

*From a painting in the National
Portrait Gallery*

WILLIAM, Duke of Clarence, afterwards William IV, was the third and least brilliant of George III's seven surviving sons. He had entered the Navy at an early age and in the course of a career in which he earned the approval and friendship of Lord Nelson, he became an exceedingly efficient naval officer. For the higher commands he was unfortunately unfitted owing to a certain streak of eccentricity in his character. Although his relations with his father were not always of the happiest, he was never actuated by that bitter animosity which rendered his elder brothers' quarrels with the King so particularly painful, and in later life was a most dutiful son. In politics his contemporaries were hard put to it to discover from the evidence of his frequent speeches in the House of Lords which party he supported. Unlike the Duke of Cumberland he was far from being an uncompromising Tory, but on the other hand he had no sympathy with the extreme Whiggery of the Dukes of Kent and Sussex. If he is judged by his actions after he became King, he will probably be accounted a moderate Whig.

In 1817 the Prince Regent's only child, the Princess Charlotte, died in childbirth, and the Duke of Clarence was prevailed upon to quit the semi-retired state in which he had hitherto lived in order to marry and secure the succession. The bride to whom he was finally married in 1818 was a Princess Adelaide of Saxe-Meiningen, a devout but nervous woman who achieved a quite incomprehensible unpopularity at the time of the passage of the Reform Bill.

As a king, William IV was, at his accession in 1830, immensely popular. This was largely due to his unassuming character which, coupled with his well-known dislike of ceremonial and display, rendered him an agreeable contrast to George IV.

The burning political question of the day was Parliamentary Reform, and when the Whigs came into power in 1831 its solution could no longer be postponed. The passage of the Bill through the Commons was as certain as its rejection by the Lords, and it soon became apparent that the only means by which the opposition of the Upper House could be overcome was by a wholesale creation of peers. This William IV at first refused to sanction, but when the Tories had been given the opportunity to form a Government, which they found themselves unable to take, he readily recalled the Whigs and undertook to persuade a majority of the Lords to drop their opposition to the Bill, which was finally passed by a small majority.

His refusal at first to agree to the creation of additional Whig peers, which was actually due to his praiseworthy sense of caution, was generally attributed to lukewarmness in support of Reform, and for a time he forfeited some of his original popularity.

For the rest of his reign the King led a happy domestic life with his devoted wife, diversified by frequent public appearances, on which occasions he found an agreeable outlet for his natural garrulity in interminable flights of official oratory, and only slightly clouded by his relations with his sister-in-law the Duchess of Kent, a German Princess in whom the consciousness of being the mother of the future Queen frequently overcame a small reserve of tact. He died quietly on June 20th, 1837, with the somewhat cryptic remark, " The Church, the Church ! "

Although in some ways one of the least remarkable of our kings, it is to William IV's eternal credit that it was in his reign, and largely due to his merits, that the English Monarchy passed comparatively scathless through a period of great danger which elsewhere proved disastrous. He may not have been a clever man, but he was the only European king who had so far survived the advent of Democracy.

VICTORIA
1837-1901

*From a painting by Thomas Sully
in the Wallace Collection*

ON her accession in 1837 Victoria had little save her youth and innocence, both however valuable assets in a generation which set a premium on sentimentality, to recommend her to her subjects. The prestige of the royal family was far from high, for although William IV, unlike his brother, had been regarded by his people with a certain degree of affection, they had never accorded him much respect, and in a society grown moral over-night, Victoria's various uncles were undoubtedly a heavy liability. Moreover, the influence which her maternal relatives (more particularly her uncle, King Leopold of the Belgians) were popularly credited with exercising at court, was generally resented, and it may be doubted whether her marriage to her first cousin, Prince Albert of Saxe-Coburg and Gotha, in 1841 did much to increase her popularity.

The Coburgs were a family of minor German royalty who by means of a contemporary outlook, considerable financial astuteness and a series of judicious marriages, contrived to worm their way on to half the thrones of Europe, where they fulfilled the nineteenth century's conception of the perfect monarch as successfully as Louis XIV had done that of the eighteenth. Prince Albert was a typical member of his family, intelligent, excessively industrious and resolutely interfering, but luckily his moral standards were considerably higher than those of many of his relations, and he proved himself a good husband and steadying influence for the young Queen. Tactless, serious and very German, it must be confessed that he endeared himself to no one save his wife, and at the time of the Crimean War, for which the nation had long been clamouring and which he regarded as certainly unnecessary and probably dangerous, his unpopularity attained formidable proportions ; needless to say, the fact that the outcome of this disastrous campaign proved him right and the war party wrong, did little to restore him to favour. Foiled by Palmerston in his repeated attempts to direct the country's foreign policy, Albert turned his attention to internal affairs and there issued from his workroom a constant stream of plans, suggestions and memoranda dealing with every subject from army reform to ecclesiastical architecture, His incredible industry eventually overtaxed his strength, and when in 1861 he caught a chill at a military review. he was dead within the week. Although Prince Albert never succeeded in gaining the affection of the English he had several claims to their gratitude. Not only was he responsible for the conception and subsequent success of the Great Exhibition of 1851, that vast and rosy mirror which showed the nineteenth century to itself in the most favourable light, but he also, on the eve of his death, saved the country, by the judicious rewriting of a truculent dispatch, from an almost certain war with the northern states of America.

The effect of her husband's death on Victoria herself was overwhelming. For twenty years she had consulted him in everything, and he had largely moulded her character ; now that he was gone she abandoned herself to the wildest grief, completely cutting herself off from all contact with her people, whose lack of appreciation of Albert she seemed to regard as being in some way responsible for his death. While her soldiers and her merchants were daily increasing the size and wealth of her dominions, Victoria remained shut up with her numerous children at Osborne or Balmoral, staunchly refusing to show herself to her people or to undertake any of her public duties, but nevertheless never failing to keep a watchful and intimidating eye on the activities of her ministers, particularly in the department of foreign affairs. Despite the growing resentment of her subjects who, although quite willing to respect her grief, could see no good reason for her retirement being indefinitely prolonged, it was only with the greatest difficulty that she was at length prevailed upon in the seventies occasionally to appear again in public. However, by 1887 she was once more firmly reinstated in the affections of the nation and in that year was celebrated the Jubilee of her accession.

As the Queen drove through the streets of her capital she seemed to her cheering subjects, to many of whom her appearance had become quite unfamiliar, to be the very embodiment of their country's power and glory, which were then at their height. By reason of her vast possessions overseas, the long start she had gained in the industrial revolution, and the consequent success of the policy of Free Trade, England now occupied a more glorious position in the world than had ever before been enjoyed by a single nation. Rivals there were none, for France was still suffering from the effects of the war of 1870, Prussia had not yet attained her full strength, Russia and Austria were busy in the Balkans, and Italy had only just achieved her independence.

Ten years later, at the time of the Diamond Jubilee, although outwardly the country's position was more splendid than ever, the situation was rapidly changing. Other countries were now in a position favourably to compete with England in the markets of the world, notably Germany and the United States, and moreover the military power of the former was fast becoming a menace that none could afford to ignore. In a world of young and vigorous nations greedy for colonies and prestige, England now occupied a position of isolation which may have been glorious but was certainly precarious. Among the aged Queen's numerous grandsons, sons-in-law and cousins occupying a variety of European thrones, who now followed her carriage to St. Paul's, there were several who, despite their respectful and affectionate bearing, entertained feelings that were far from friendly towards the land she ruled. Victoria's last years were saddened by the outbreak and initial disasters of the Boer War, the successful conclusion of which she did not live to see. She died at Osborne in 1901, aged eighty-two.

Few monarchs have stamped their personalities so firmly on the age in which they lived as Queen Victoria. Hers was a shrewd and practical intelligence, and in dealing with the manifold problems which presented themselves in the course of her long life, she was constantly saved from disaster by the exercise of a formidable commonsense. Her reign, the longest in English history, coincided with a period of vast and rapid changes in which her country's fortunes reached their zenith, and gradually her people came to identify their Queen with the power and prosperity which they then enjoyed. Finally, the firmness of her character, the fearful dignity of her bearing, her great age, and even her limitations which the majority of her subjects shared and regarded rather as virtues, caused Victoria to appear not only to her own people but to the whole world as a more than human figure, a species of tribal divinity, and her reign a Golden, but far from pagan, Age.

EDWARD VII
1901-1910

Published by permission of
W. and D. Downey

EDWARD VII 1901—1910

ON the death of the aged Queen in 1901 there were many who regarded the person of her successor with a certain degree of anxiety. Although Edward VII was then sixty he had had no practical experience of government or administration, as his indomitable mother had always refused to allow him to share in any way the burdens of her office; she was determined that those privileges which she had been forced to refuse Albert she would not lightly accord to his son, whom she considered had not yet exhibited in a sufficiently marked degree those qualities of balance and austerity for which his lamented father had been so justly famous. However, her judgment and that of those of her subjects who agreed with her, was gravely at fault, for Edward VII soon displayed a skill and ability in dealing both with his ministers and with foreign powers that justly caused him to be regarded as the most enlightened of contemporary monarchs.

In 1902 the Boer War, which had afforded the War Office an opportunity for displaying a heroic incompetence such as they had not enjoyed since the days of the Crimea, was brought to a negotiated and honourable conclusion, but unluckily there was no corresponding improvement in the European situation. England's isolated position was now more marked even than it had been five years earlier; no continental nation, with

the honourable exception of Italy, had made any effort
to conceal its sympathy with the Boers and nearly all
had concrete reasons for their antagonism ; our relations with Russia had always been bad and were at the
moment rendered worse by conflicting interests in Persia
and Central Asia ; the occupation of Egypt and
colonial rivalry in Africa had alienated the never very
warm sympathies of the French. The menacing attitude
of Germany, which was the most dangerous aspect of
the whole situation, sprang from causes more personal
and more complicated, of which the mutual antipathy
existing between King Edward and his nephew the
Kaiser was not the least. The latter, who had from
his youth exhibited a lack of balance startling in one
who could claim Victoria as a grandmother, was obsessed
by a feeling for England in general and his uncle in particular that was half hatred, half admiration and wholly
irrational, and which filled him with an urgent desire
to assert himself on every occasion. Had he been content to emulate King Edward's urbanity and taste in
clothes all would have been well, but unfortunately his
envy was aroused by his uncle's navy even more than
by his social graces. As a result Germany embarked
on a programme of naval construction that if it continued unchecked seemed likely not only to threaten
England's maritime predominance but endanger her
very existence as a first-rate power. Faced with such
a prospect as this it now became imperative for this
country to improve her relations with France, and the
fact that this difficult feat was successfully accomplished

was largely the outcome of King Edward's initiative and diplomacy.

At the general election of 1905 the Liberals returned to power with an overwhelming majority and at once prepared to introduce fiscal and educational measures more comprehensive and far-reaching than any previous legislation. One by one these bills, having passed the Commons, were rejected by the House of Lords, and it became obvious that Mr. Asquith, who had succeeded to the leadership of the Liberal party on the death of Mr. Campbell-Bannerman, would be forced to take drastic steps if the Government was to have any legislative achievements to its credit at all. The King now indicated to his ministers that before he would give any undertaking to exercise his royal powers in order to overcome the opposition of the Upper House, there must be a further appeal to the country ; accordingly another election was held in 1910, as a result of which the Liberals returned once more, but so sadly reduced in numbers that they were compelled to rely on the support of the Irish Nationalists, an unscrupulous and cynical body of men who for the sake of Home Rule would willingly have sold their own mothers. However, before the battle could open in real earnest King Edward died, and so great had his reputation as a diplomatist and liaison officer between conflicting parties now become that even among the Liberals, sorrow for his death far outweighed annoyance at the inconvenience it caused.

Although he was a Coburg by birth, had received a typical Coburg education and was markedly Coburg in appearance, Edward VII was in many ways a true Hanoverian. He had inherited all the shrewdness, social gifts and interest in the minutiæ of masculine attire that were characteristic of that family, but in addition to these estimable qualities he also possessed a marked consideration for the welfare of others, a virtue with which few of its members had been overburdened. With the middle classes his popularity was never as great as his mother's, but with the upper and lower strata of society even greater; his affability, his dandyism, his sporting activities and his indiscretions all served to render him a familiar and beloved figure not only to the man about town but also to the man in the street.

But of all his qualities the most praiseworthy and the most memorable was his fanatical love of peace. Again and again he showed his eagerness to avoid war and to mitigate its barbarities if it proved to be unavoidable; and it was this fervid hatred of war which impressed itself on the public more forcibly than any of his other characteristics.

> As long as there's a king like good King Edward,
> There'll be no wars ;
> 'E 'ates that sort of thing.

The ironic reflection that the system of alliances on which the eccentricities of his unreliable nephew forced him to embark only helped to render inevitable a conflict more terrible even than he feared, should not blind us to his disinterested and ceaseless striving for international tranquillity.

GEORGE V
1910-1936

GEORGE V 1910—1936

FEW modern kings have been faced at their accession with so complicated and so threatening a situation as that which confronted King George V. The political crisis which had arisen at the end of the last reign now assumed the most dangerous aspect and never before had the two great political parties been divided by such bitter and such irreconcilable differences. Once more a sailor king was called upon to give assurances to his Whig ministers that in the event of the House of Lords persisting in their opposition to the Government's schemes for constitutional reform, he would create the required number of Liberal peers ; once more the Upper House, when faced with the steady determination of their sovereign to abide by the constitution and the advice of his government, shrank from the prospect of " dying in the last ditch " and passed the measure. However, the Liberals had had to pay a high price for their victory, for in order to pass their Bill through the Commons they had been forced to bribe the Irish members with the promise of Home Rule : a promise the redemption of which brought the country nearer to Civil War than it had come at any time since 1688.

On the eve of 1914 the internal situation had become almost desperate. Despite the bitter opposition of the Protestant North, the Liberal Government, whose credit had been somewhat shaken by an unsavoury financial scandal, persisted in its intention of forcing through a Home Rule Bill which placed the whole of Ireland, including Ulster, in the hands of the Irish Nationalists. Had it come to an open struggle, Mr. Asquith and his party would have been hard put to it to enforce their decrees, for the Ulstermen, under the leadership of Carson and F. E. Smith, were preparing to defend their position by force of arms, the Conservatives were united in their support and many of the army chiefs were openly disloyal. Nor were these the only difficulties with which the country was faced, for during 1912 and 1913 a succession of bitter and prolonged strikes had shattered the peace of the industrial world, while the daily life of the nation was continually being harassed and disorganized by the policy of intimidation and outrage embarked on by the militant suffragettes. However, by the end of July, 1914, all these dangers had paled into insignificance beside the threatening aspect of the situation abroad. The heir to the throne of Austria had been assassinated at the end of June by a Serbian fanatic, and so half-hearted and inefficient had been the efforts to localize the struggle which this outrage was inevitably bound to provoke, that it had now become obvious that England, together with half the nations of Europe, was certain to be involved in a desperate war in which King George's position would be one of peculiar difficulty, for not only was he a first cousin of both the Kaiser and the Czar, but he was also closely related to the King of the Belgians and many of the German princes.

The war of 1914-1918, which rapidly developed into

the bitterest and most disastrous conflict in which the nations had engaged since the wars of religion, was notable both for the lack of military genius displayed by the various commanders (it produced no Napoleon, no Marlborough, no Moltke), and for the fact that it was fought not by highly trained professional armies but by whole nations in arms. At first both sides were equally confident that the war would be over in a few months, but as winter succeeded autumn and spring winter, it became obvious that the struggle would be both exhausting and prolonged. All through these dreary and agonizing years, the King worked as selflessly and as hard as any of his subjects ; not only did he resolutely fulfil the manifold duties of his position, now more numerous and more arduous than ever, but also found time frequently to visit his troops both at home and at the front. At length, in the late autumn of 1918, Austria having already collapsed, Germany, on the failure of her own last effort to bring the war to a successful conclusion before the Allies should have gained the full benefit of America's intervention, was forced to sue for peace, and an armistice was signed.

The peace negotiations which followed were almost as prolonged, fully as futile and conducted with even more bitterness than the hostilities which they brought to an end.

In England the years which followed the war were ones of industrial strife, endless troubles with Ireland and slow, very slow economic recovery. As a result of the general election of 1924 the Socialists took office for the first time, and the smoothness and lack of friction attendant on their assumption of power was due in a large measure to the tact and intelligence of the King. It is reported that he replied in answer to a question as to his relations with his new ministers, " My grandmother would have hated them, my father would not have understood them, but I find that I get along with them very well." In 1926, when the Conservatives were once more in power, there occurred a General Strike, the failure of which proved that the coming of the motor-car and the wireless had done much to deprive a measure which had hitherto always been regarded as the prelude to revolution of much of its effectiveness.

The period 1926–1931 was one in which all touch with reality both in the economic and financial spheres seems to have been lost. As a result of the prevailing prosperity, which rested on the shakiest foundations, there was everywhere, but more particularly in America, a tremendous increase in speculation of the most fantastic sort : currencies, commodities, stocks and shares were all valued at prices which bore no relation at all to their real worth. At the end of the twenties came the inevitable collapse. Germany, who had been forced at the Peace Conference to engage herself to pay to the Allies reparations assessed by them at almost astronomical figures, had been bled white and could now no longer pay even the amounts to which her obligations had been finally reduced, whereupon the Allies defaulted on the payment of their own debts to the United States, which had been calculated on a similarly fantastic basis. As a

result the boom-period in America came to an abrupt
end and the effects of this sudden collapse were immediately appalling and soon became universal. Hundreds
of banks were forced to shut their doors, everywhere the
numbers of the unemployed rapidly increased and trade
was at a standstill. When the full force of the storm hit
England in 1931 the Socialist Government which was
then in power, showed itself quite incapable, under the
leadership of Mr. Macdonald, of dealing with the situation, and a serious crisis arose. At this moment, when
his ministers were displaying a tendency to panic, King
George at once took the initiative; summoning the
leaders of the three parties to the palace he urged upon
them the necessity of forming the national coalition
government which obtained an overwhelming majority
at the subsequent election. This was the last great crisis
of the King's reign, and five years later he celebrated his
Silver Jubilee amid scenes of quite unparalleled enthusiasm, and in eight months he was dead.

Although he had little of that easy affability and
personal picturesqueness that had made his father so
popular a figure, George V was accorded by his subjects
a degree of affection and respect to which few of his
predecessors could lay claim. The uprightness and
simplicity of his private life, his fondness for outdoor
sports and his love and faithful observance of tradition
all served to endear him to his people. The development
of broadcasting in the latter part of his reign placed the
whole relationship of monarch and subject on a more
intimate basis and gave to the King's position as the one

great link between all parts of his wide Empire a new and personal significance. The sound of the King's voice, which had a quality of personal sincerity that was infinitely moving, broadcast round the world probably did more than any other single event in our recent history to strengthen the position of the Crown and established in the minds of all who heard it the conviction that here was a sovereign who, despite his remarkable skill in adapting himself to changing conditions of life, would never for one moment compromise with his exalted conception of the dignity and obligations of kingship.

EDWARD VIII
1936

Published by permission of " The Times "

EDWARD VIII 1936

WHEN Edward VIII arrived by air in his capital in 1936 he enjoyed one great advantage that had been denied his father a quarter of a century earlier ; his character and appearance were both thoroughly familiar to the subjects whom he had been called upon to rule. Whereas George V at the time of his accession was comparatively unknown, both at home and abroad, his son had visited not only every quarter of his vast empire but also a wide range of foreign capitals ; had made the acquaintance of not only the most prominent persons of the time but also numberless individuals drawn from the less exalted ranks of his future subjects. Moreover, his familiarity with all the numerous grades of the pyramidical society of which he was the apex was not confined to times of peace, for he had been a witness of the participation of all classes in the great struggle which had dominated the world during his youth. Unlike the late King, who had become heir-apparent only on the death of his brother, which occurred when he was already grown up, King Edward had been born in the direct line of succession and so had his whole life to prepare himself for the great office he would one day hold. While his education had been the most thorough ever enjoyed by an heir to the throne, it had been founded on more liberal principles and had been characterized by a more practical grasp of the problems to be faced than that which the Prince Consort had inflicted on the unfortunate Edward VII.

George V had married in 1893 Princess Mary of Teck, a granddaughter of that Duke of Cambridge who had been the youngest son of George III, a woman of great character and dignity who had always displayed the highest qualities as a Queen, as a wife and as a mother, and for whom her own family and the nation at large had always entertained feelings of the deepest affection and respect. Under the guidance of his parents the young prince was gradually acquainted with various aspects of the task which would one day confront him, while at the same time every effort was made to render his youth as normal as it was possible for that of a future monarch to be. He was sent to Magdalen College, Oxford, and when war broke out entered the army and saw active service in France. However, unlike so many of his German cousins of the same age who were given the commands of armies where their presence only served to embarrass their staffs while contributing little to the efficiency of their various units, the Prince of Wales carried out his duties as a junior officer under conditions which approximated as closely as was possible to those of normal active service (despite his eagerness to remain constantly in the firing line it was manifestly impossible to expose the heir to the throne to the risk, not of death, but of capture). After the war he made numerous tours to the dominions, to India and to foreign countries, and at the time of his accession he was undoubtedly the most travelled monarch who ever ascended a throne.

In addition to this extensive experience of distant lands, he had acquired a wide knowledge of the conditions prevailing in the industrial areas at home, which had led him to interest himself particularly in the problems of housing, and he became one of the most tireless advocates of an enlightened policy of planning and modernization. His concern for the welfare of the poorer classes in general and the unemployed in particular was deep and practical, and his action in subscribing to the Miners' Relief Fund during the great coal strike testified to the independence of his judgment and endeared him personally to the most radical section of the population. Few kings at their accession had already earned the loyalty and goodwill of the nation in so remarkable a degree—few kings have availed themselves of these advantages for so short a time.

Even before the death of George V rumours had circulated concerning an unfortunate attachment which the Prince had formed, and after his father's death these rumours increased in volume and fantasy. The British Press with a meritorious unanimity refrained from reference or comment, but the American newspapers were under no obligation to exercise a similar restraint and as the object of the Royal affections, a certain Mrs. Simpson, was of American origin, the exhaustive nature of their published revelations was only exceeded by their intimacy. In the autumn of 1936 a further and more disturbing rumour was current that the new King intended to marry the lady, and by the beginning of December it had become apparent that both Press and

Parliament would shortly be forced to take some cognizance of the affair. Finally the storm broke more or less by chance; certain North of England newspapers attributed to a speech by the Bishop of Bradford a significance of which that prelate was himself unaware and the country found itself involved overnight in a first-class constitutional crisis.

Some time previously the King had intimated to the Prime Minister, Mr. Baldwin, his intention to make this Mrs. Simpson his wife and it now became obvious that there were four courses open to him. He could marry the lady and make her queen, he could contract a morganatic marriage in which case she would not be queen, he could abdicate and marry her or he could abandon the whole project. To each of these courses save the last there were grave objections. That the intended queen was a commoner and an American would not, in these democratic times, have been regarded as an obstacle; moreover, Edward IV and Henry VIII had both married commoners, but the fact that Mrs. Simpson had divorced two husbands both of whom were still living, although there did in fact exist a precedent for a divorcée queen (Eleanor of Aquitaine's first husband was still alive at the time of her marriage to Henry II), was one that the majority of the nation would not accept. On the other hand, there did not exist in English law any such thing as a morganatic marriage and therefore special legislation would have had to be introduced, which Parliament and the Dominion Governments would undoubtedly refuse to initiate. Therefore the King was forced to choose between the renunciation of his project and abdication. At first it seemed possible that he might obtain a certain measure of support which would enable him to override the advice of his ministers ; he was personally immensely popular with a large section of the nation, he had the support of one or two newspapers and there existed a feeling in certain quarters that he was being unfairly bullied by the Government. But as the crisis wore on the alarming prospect of the formation of a king's party vanished utterly, for it soon became known that the Government had put no compulsion on the King, that the Opposition was behind them in their handling of the affair and that popular as the King was the standards of conduct of the Fort Belvedere circle were as alien to the great bulk of the nation as they were unacceptable to the Church. Accordingly on 10th of December, 1936, to the genuine regret of the majority of his subjects, King Edward VIII announced his intention to abdicate. On the following night he broadcast his farewell to the whole Empire and immediately left for the Continent.

Edward VIII was a Prince in whom the charm and affability of the Hanoverians were rather more conspicuous than the judgment and discretion of the Coburgs. No one questioned the fact that the private life of the sovereign was his own affair provided that it remained private. While he had inherited many of the characteristics of his grandfather, Edward VIII found himself unable to emulate that monarch's discretion, and owing either to a mistaken estimate of the popular feeling or to a highly creditable but unfortunate longing for the pleasures of domesticity was induced to place his personal problem on a plane where it automatically became a matter of national importance.

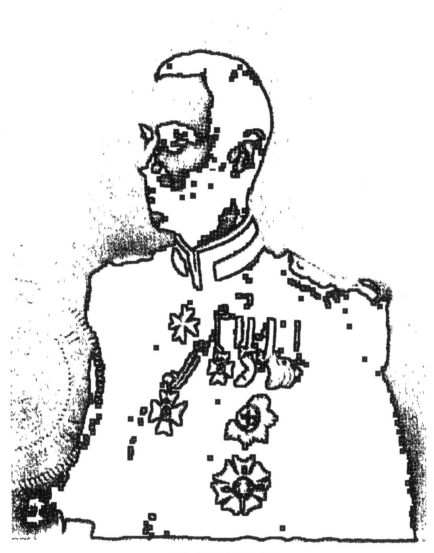

GEORGE VI
1936

*From a photograph by Speaight Ltd., London,
by courtesy of Messrs. Hutchinson*

WHEN it was learnt that Edward VIII was to be succeeded by his brother the Duke of York the country experienced a deep feeling of relief. George V's second son, although not very well known to the majority of his new subjects, was generally considered to have inherited many of those admirable and steady virtues which had so distinguished his beloved father. Moreover, his education and upbringing had followed similar lines ; both father and son had been born out of the direct line of succession and neither had therefore been prepared for the high office that they subsequently held, and both had entered the navy as boys in the ordinary way. It is frequently but erroneously stated that George II was the last of our sovereigns to take part in a battle whereas he was actually only the last to take part in a military engagement. Until the accession of George VI, William IV had been the last who could claim this distinction by virtue of his naval service during the Napoleonic Wars. The new King has served his country in almost exactly similar conditions ; while still Prince Albert he had been present at the battle of Jutland on board H.M.S. *Collingwood*, and had played his part as a member of the gun team in the forward turret. Although this was not his only experience of active service, he was compelled by almost constant ill health while afloat finally to leave the navy

Lightning Source UK Ltd.
Milton Keynes UK
UKHW031836200821
389183UK00008B/1427